Evolutionary Processes and Organizational Adaptation

Evolutionary Processes and Organizational Adaptation

*A Mendelian Perspective on
Strategic Management*

Daniel A. Levinthal

OXFORD
UNIVERSITY PRESS

OXFORD
UNIVERSITY PRESS

Great Clarendon Street, Oxford, OX2 6DP,
United Kingdom

Oxford University Press is a department of the University of Oxford.
It furthers the University's objective of excellence in research, scholarship,
and education by publishing worldwide. Oxford is a registered trade mark of
Oxford University Press in the UK and in certain other countries

First Edition published in 2021

Impression: 2

Published in the United States of America by Oxford University Press
198 Madison Avenue, New York, NY 10016, United States of America

British Library Cataloguing in Publication Data
Data available

Library of Congress Control Number: 2021938122

ISBN 978–0–19–968494–6

Printed and bound by
CPI Group (UK) Ltd, Croydon, CR0 4YY

Acknowledgments

While academic endeavors are often thought of as rather solitary efforts, that is a very partial and largely false image. However far I may have proceeded down the particular path I have traveled, it was with the insight, inspiration, and support of family, friends, and collaborators—which have been nicely overlapping sets. Indeed, significant elements of the work come directly from prior collaborations and are acknowledged as such in the text. Further, some members of the friends and collaborators categories, Ron Adner, Giovanni Gavetti, Thorbjørn Knudsen, and Phanish Puranam, engaged in the particular gift of commenting on prior drafts of the manuscript. The quixotic (and somewhat bold and arrogant) enterprise of engaging in a substantial piece of research can not be sustained without steadfast support, support in my case that was seemingly blind and non-adaptive to the interminable delays in the production of this work. I am deeply grateful to this wonderful community of support. In particular, I appreciated the intermittent inquirers from my sons Asher and Adam, and partner Lisa, about "how the book was going" that conveyed support of the project without judgment regarding it's rate of progress. I want to single out a particular member of this community who is both ever-present and no longer with us. I wish to dedicate the work to James G. March, from whom I learned much of life, models, and organizations.

Contents

Introduction

A self-consciously behavioral approach to organizations has, if not its literal beginnings, certainly its foundational touchstone in the "Carnegie School" as put forward in the work of March and Simon (1958) and Cyert and March (1963). The program put forward some central behavioral postulates at the individual level of bounded rationality and the role of search in problem-solving, and for organizations the dual challenges of coordination and cooperation. Two decades later, Nelson and Winter (1982) offered up another important conceptual platform, an evolutionary theory of organizations and industry. While broadly sympathetic to the Carnegie School, Nelson and Winter were less focused on decision-making, the central unit of analysis for Simon (1947), than the nature of knowledge (Polyani, 1964). The tacit and localized nature of knowledge, which Nelson and Winter developed in their concept of routines, formed the core theoretical argument for the stable heterogeneity in capabilities among firms, which in turn underlie their analysis of industry dynamics.

We now appear to be experiencing a third epoch, one less driven by theoretical advances but rather by management practice and helpful "engineers" of these practices of experimentation and pivoting (Blank, 2003; Reis, 2011). In some sense, this brings us back full circle to the work of the Carnegie School for which search and learning are the central mechanisms of interest. However, this "return" has a degree of intentionality and self-conscious design that this earlier work lacked or certainly did not highlight. Indeed, some variants of these experimental efforts, such as the use of random controlled trials (RCTs) and "big data" and AI-based learning algorithms, appear to approximate a kind of "behavioral rationality." That is, in contrast to neoclassical expressions of rational choice, there is a considerable emphasis on uncertainty and the role of learning; but, at the same time, this learning process is presumed to have something akin to a modern Taylorism of engineered trials. There is both promise and challenges with these approaches. While the image of a startup pivoting to product-market fit and subsequently scaling is compelling, it is important to consider what constitutes these adjacent markets and technologies and what is the selection process that serves as a catalyst to scaling. The experimental approach of RCTs and the inferential engine of "big data" and A.I.-based learning algorithms are challenging in the context of strategic actions, where the immediate feedback may not be strongly indicative of longer-run outcomes of interest. It is exciting to see a growing interest in learning in the world of practice, but also of some concern to see the encroachment of some forms of the hubris of rationality to which the Carnegie School provided a rebuttal and an alternative pathway forward. While behavioralism does not negate conscious choice and some degree of anticipation of the consequences of those choices (Gavetti and Levinthal, 2000), it is important to remain mindful of their limits.

The current work in some sense is an amalgam of these three broad approaches. Building on the strong shoulders of Nelson and Winter, it takes an explicitly evolutionary perspective on organizational change. As Campbell (1965) long ago noted, and Knudsen and Hodgeson (2010) have more recently elaborated, a generalized Darwinian perspective can be usefully applied to non-biological social systems. This work takes a further step away from the biological in that it foregoes the concept of a gene or any analogous construct. The notion of a "gene" creates some fundamental problems (i.e. baggage) in the consideration of organizations; and in particular raises questions such as what is the analog of a genetic endowment and what is a "generation" in an organizational context?

As elaborated in the following chapters, an evolutionary perspective can be a powerful guide even in the absence of these more literal biological mechanisms. What is central from the perspective developed here is that behaviors in the near future are guided by and constrained by behaviors in the near past. This is not a postulate of inertia, but rather merely of some form of path-dependence. The second central prop that the work takes from evolutionary theory, particularly as developed by Winter (1964) and Nelson and Winter

(1982), is that competitive forces of selection are real and are quite powerful; but, at the same time, they are not the "magic wand" of stylized accounts of competitive dynamics that suggest some near instantaneous shift to equilibrium outcomes. Selection is a statement of relative fitness and therefore depends on the set of organizations in the current population, not some latent best-possible form. Further, competitive processes even among the extant population play out over time.

The non-instantaneous nature of selection allows for some loose coupling between the nature of these external forces and the rewards structures and resource allocation mechanisms the organization chooses to impose. These later properties are referred to as the organization's *artificial selection environment*. The modifier "artificial" is used to indicate that these selection rules are the product of conscious choice and not directly the by-product of competitive consequences of market processes. There are two basic challenges that an artificial selection process faces: one is temporal and the other is spatial.

The temporal facet is that signals of fitness or performance today may not be strongly indicative of fitness or performance of those same initiatives at some future point—whether because the external environment may change so as to become more or less receptive to the initiative or because the initiative itself goes though some developmental process of change and elicits different feedback even if the environment has remain fixed. This possible loose coupling between current external selection forces and the artificial selection regime specified within the organization allows for strategic vision, risk-taking, and foolishness. As March (2006) notes, those qualities are difficult to distinguish ex ante. An issue highlighted in the discussion developed here is that even the markers of what might constitute desired performance become objects of contestation and conjecture.

The other challenge, spatial, stems from the basic imperative for forming organizations in the first place and that is the possible benefits of collective action and coordination of disparate individuals through an organizational form. The specialization and coordination of effort, and the associated joint production, are fundamental to the rationale for formal organizations (Smith, 1776; Alchian and Demsetz, 1972; Williamson, 1975). However, these same attributes make the allocation of rewards to individual actors within organizations problematic. As Gibbons (1999) observes, markets take the "easy" problems where coordination is less problematic, and leave the "hard" problems for organizations. The imperfect enactment of reward structures to address the dual challenges of cooperation and coordination (Puranam, 2018) that organizations face is another critical facet of this artificial selection. Agency models tend to highlight the challenge of cooperation—or as expressed in that literature the challenge of incentive conflict (Holmstrom, 2017). However, even if one puts aside the challenge of intrinsic motivational differences among actors, the challenge of aligning behavior and coordinating collective action to some shared, though typically not very operational, superordinate goal of profits is immense. As the number of actors expands and their web of interrelationships broaden and the intertemporal linkages through path-dependence deepen, projecting onto individuals and individual initiatives the more aggregate rewards experienced by the organization becomes more problematic.

There are many more steps that follow, but these are the broad contours. These steps do not lead to a fully integrative theoretical framework, but it is hoped that the work bridges some of the key ideas within the evolutionary and broader behavioral tradition and provide some further scaffolding with which to consider some of the basic challenges of organizational adaptation. It is an admittedly incomplete scaffolding and it is hoped that others will add more mass and definition to this structure.

1

Mendelian Executive

Design and the Evolution of Strategies

In our efforts to understand organizations, the strategies they enact, and the outcomes they experience, we have two broad classes of explanation: one is premised on the calculative choice of rational actors and the other on a process of evolutionary dynamics, a process of descent with variation and a contested selection process. These explanatory "poles" are fairly well defined and operate as powerful intellectual attractors. This book is an effort to construct a middle ground between these two conceptions, although adhering closer to the evolutionary "pole." Gregor Mendel is a useful touchstone for this "middle-ground."[1] Mendel did not, in some deterministic manner, specify the attributes of each generation of a lineage of peas, but rather he created conscious manipulations of the stochastic reproductive process. In the modern parlance of lean start-ups, we might think of him as specifying a series of "A/B" trials running fairly controlled experiments of local modifications and observing their effect.

The concept of a "Mendelian" executive suggests how we might link the images of godlike rational design on the one hand with evolutionary dynamics on the other. Perhaps, to some degree, we can engineer these evolutionary processes. This "Mendelian executive" operates with intentionality; but, unlike the conception of rationality in neoclassical economics, this intentionality is limited

[1] While the idea of cross-breeding of animals and plants in search of the cultivation of desired traits has been broadly understood since ancient times, Mendel, an Augustine friar working in the mid-nineteenth century, in his experiments with cross-breeding different lineages of peas laid out the genetic basis for heredity and in particular the idea of dominant and recessive traits. The appendix to this chapter provides a fuller biography of Mendel, giving some greater detail about his scientific efforts and, intriguingly, ways in which his own career has parallels to the general theoretical argument developed here.

in that the emphasis is more on the design of experimental processes rather than the design of specific paths forward. This intentionality and design set the Mendelian executive apart from a pure Darwinian process: the strategist is conceived neither as a blind watchmaker (Dawkins, 1987) nor as a chess grandmaster. The intentionality of the Mendelian executive allows for the conscious exploration of opportunities rather than the happenstance of random variants; but, the constraining forces of path-dependence tend to restrict these moves to adjacent spaces. Further, the argument developed here highlights the role of intentionality with respect to the selection and culling of strategic initiatives. The organization is viewed as operating an "artificial selection" environment in contrast to selection as the direct consequence of the outcome of competitive processes. While market outcomes may inform this artificial selection process, the two criteria need not be tightly coupled.

1.1 Twin Blades of Evolutionary Dynamics: Path-Dependence and Artificial Selection

The notion of descent with modification is central to evolutionary arguments (Darwin, 1859). This perspective has been shown to be applicable not only to biological organisms, but to non-biological entities, and in particular organizations (Aldrich, 1999; Campbell, 1965; Knudsen and Hodgeson, 2010). Campbell's framework of variation-selection-retention supplies the basic template that has informed the application of these ideas in the social sciences. Yet, the application of a framework developed in the context of evolutionary biology toward understanding the pattern of adaptation and change within human organizations poses the significant challenge of identifying parallel constructions and mechanisms in the two domains.

Particularly difficult challenges have revolved around the questions as to what constitutes a "gene" in the organizational context and, relatedly, what constitutes a "generation" in this setting. The argument developed here frees itself from this conceptual Gordian knot by offering a different set of primitives: path-dependence and artificial selection. For an evolutionary process to be a useful lens to bring the dynamics of organizations into focus, it must be the case that the current characteristics of the organization constrain, and to some degree foreshadow, the future set of characteristics. Absent this property, there would be no (semi) stable sources of heterogeneity over which the process of differential selection could operate (Levinthal, 1991a). However, the presence of path-dependence need not require relatively fixed imprinting as suggested by the construct of a gene. Another critical distinctive feature of the evolution of organizations, in contrast to biological evolutionary processes, is that organizations may constitute "artificial" selection environments in which initiatives, people, and resources can be allocated (Aldrich, 1999; Levinthal and Warglien, 1999; Lovas and Ghoshal, 2000; Levinthal and Marino, 2015). Ideas, business plans, and design efforts do not themselves directly receive rewards from the market. Firms as a whole receive profits and losses, but the firm, in turn, is able to mediate how these environmental outcomes are projected onto underlying elements of the organization. Individuals only receive rewards as mediated by an organization's accounting system and incentive structure. In this sense, a firm can be considered to be a credit assignment mechanism (Holland, 1975). At its most basic level, the firm can be viewed as part of a multi-level selection process, with an internal ecology of initiatives within the firm and the firm itself operating in a broader, macro ecology of other entities.

Mendel pointed to the underlying mechanisms that allowed him to shift the patterns of heredity, though not directly to control individual outcome. According to the framework developed in this volume, he enacted an "artificial" selection environment.[2] In the organization context, artificial selection environments can be loosely coupled to the firm's current "natural" environment of product market competition and financial market valuation processes. This

---

[2] In this regard, it is interesting to note that Darwin, in order to motivate his arguments for natural selection in his introductory chapter to the *Origin of the Species*, used the example of breeders and the cultivation of distinct traits in the animals being bred. However, Darwin was unaware of the parallel efforts of Mendel that ultimately provided the critical foundation for the genetic basis of heredity.

loose coupling allows for discretion (Burgelman, 1991; Lovas and Ghoshal, 1999) as the strategy and actions of the enterprise are not a direct consequence of external contingencies. As a consequence, this loose coupling provides a potential role for foresight (Gavetti, 2012)—for engaging in initiatives whose merit is not self-evident based on current circumstances. Of course, it also allows for the possibility of stubbornness and foolishness (March, 1994). The arguments developed here point to the role of experimentation and the broader management of the internal ecology of the organization as a partial substitute for foresight.

The focus is on the organization as the primary unit of analysis. However, organizations are neither unitary entities, nor isolated economic islands of activity. Organizations are a complex ecology of people, initiatives, cultural traits, and formal structures. These complex entities are generally embedded in a web of relationships of partners, customers, suppliers, regulators, and other classes of actors. These sets of relationships inform the dual processes of path-dependence and directed selection. As result of both these rich internal and external structures, it is important to engage with multiple levels of analysis.

However, there remains an important question as to what constitutes the unit of selection in such processes. A strategy is generally taken to be a holistic perspective on the way in which a firm competes, with a "parts-whole" sensibility being central in classic writings as to what constitutes a firm strategy (Andrews, 1971; Porter, 1996). In that regard, an experimental approach appears problematic. An experiment of repositioning an overall enterprise is a "bet the company" move, not a "trial." As a result, an experimental approach lends itself more naturally to the development of technologies, products, and novel services than to an overarching strategy. However, as Andrews (1971) observed in his work that has served as an early touchstone for the strategy field, strategy-making is, to a large degree, enacted by the resource allocation across competing initiatives within the enterprise, a process in turn guided by the criteria for resource allocation and the overarching decision premises (Simon, 1976 [1947]) put forth by top management. In that light, as Andrews (1971) suggests, strategy can be viewed as a pattern of decision-making and resource allocation. This "pattern" is identifiable as a result of a reasonably stable logic and set of decision criteria guiding these processes. The logic may be guided by a well-posed activity system or a more diffuse sense of leveraging capabilities and resources into adjacent "spaces."

In this regard, the firm adapts at fundamentally two different levels. At a lower level, products, technologies, and markets change in response to experimentation and the feedback received both directly from the market, but also importantly as evaluated by the criteria of the firm's internal selection processes. A second, generally slower, process is the change in these criteria themselves. In this spirit, exploration can be considered not merely as the distance in the underlying behavior from current action, but also as changes in the dimensions of merit by which initiatives are judged (Adner and Levinthal, 2008; Csaszar and Levinthal, 2016).

While organizations of any scale or scope can generally sustain a wide variety of initiatives, it is more difficult to sustain a variety of selection criteria. To the extent organizations are hierarchical systems, the selection criteria will tend to reflect the beliefs of those at the apex of that hierarchy (Levinthal, 2017). As a result, for a plurality of beliefs to drive in a meaningful manner the allocation of resources, there generally needs to be some decentralization in the resource allocation process. Structural decomposition of a firm's activity can facilitate adaptation and identification of new strategies (Siggelkow and Levinthal, 2004, 2005). A less structural mechanism is organizational slack which allows for greater degrees of search and innovation (March and Simon, 1958). As part of effective design, the Mendelian executive creates structures that allow novel variants some opportunity to express themselves and to avoid screening on the basis of a singular lens.

Figure 1.1 provides a summary representation of the perspective put forth here. Mendelian executives have discretion, but that discretion is constrained by the context in which they operate. The set of possible initiatives is a function of the set of existing initiatives and resources at their disposal, as well as by their imagination of alternative possibilities, which in turn is imprinted by their particular experiences and historical context (Pontikes and Rindova, 2020).

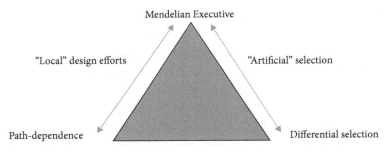

Figure 1.1 Mendelian executive and the design and evolution of strategies.

Similarly, while the Mendelian executive is capable of enacting an artificial selection environment, this artificial selection environment cannot be fully decoupled from the external selection environment in which the organization operates. At longer time intervals, the bidirectional quality of the arrows of influence takes on a greater significance. Actions taken today can impact the set of possible actions tomorrow. Path-dependence is not only a backward-looking constraint, but current actions are enabling of future possibilities. This latter possibility is highlighted in discussions of real options (Trigeorgis and Reuer, 2017). Similarly, niches not only constrain but are constructed, both individually and collectively (Odling-Smee, 2003).

We start our consideration at the level of individual actors. Even given what is unambiguously a unitary actor, an individual has a plurality of thoughts, action repertories, and bases of experience. In that regard, one can consider micro-entities underlying an individual and treat an individual as a "macro" aggregate.[3] From this perspective, Chapter 2 explores the common underlying structures of the seemingly disparate processes of choice, selection, and learning. The discussion then shifts to consider the internal ecology of an organization. While Campbell (1965) put forward the tripartite framework of variation, selection, and retention, the framework developed here is fundamentally bipartite: consisting of path-dependence and selection. This work offers an evolutionary

[3] Indeed, this has become an increasingly dominant view in work in psychology and artificial intelligence (Dennett, 1991).

perspective on organizations freed of the analogue of a gene or generation. It is sufficient for evolutionary dynamics to manifest themselves for the characteristics of a particular entity at one point in time to constrain the possible realizations at a subsequent time period. Chapter 3 examines the nature of path-dependence and extends this consideration to an examination of the concept of dynamic capabilities. The selection processes of interest here, and developed in Chapter 4, are not so much those of the market or the institutional environment, but the criteria for rewards, capital allocation, and project selection at the various levels of management within the enterprise. Chapter 5 builds on this discussion of selection criteria and revisits the exploration/exploitation tradeoff, offering an argument that exploration can be viewed as less a feature of the behavior itself and more a function of the dimensions of merit by which the behavior is evaluated. The pace of change is an important question for an evolutionary argument. Certainly, the notion of path-dependence would appear to be a strong "rate limiting" property. However, when we recognize the variegated nature of selection environments, both internal and external to the organization, even in the presence of strongly path-dependent processes, we observe seemingly radical and discrete change. This "incremental" view of seemingly punctuated change is developed in Chapter 6. Drawing on the conceptual apparatus developed in the prior chapters, Chapter 7 first contrasts the role of context dependence across different modes of experimentation, ranging from random controlled trials (RCTs), A/B testing, reinforcement learning, and processes of imitation and recombination. The chapter then concludes with some tentative suggestions for our "Mendelian executive."

Mendel

While the almost fairy-tale narrative of Mendel's life with which most of us understand his story suggests an inspired genius working in isolation coming up with the foundations of genetics, Mendel's actual biography is illustrative in some respects of the arguments developed here regarding the path-dependent moves into adjacencies that may, in some instances, create significant changes—and in the case of Mendel, scientific breakthroughs.[4]

Given his family's modest circumstances, Mendel joined a monastery as a means by which he would be able to continue his education. Fortuitously, the monastery to which he was directed was an Augustinian monastery led by an abbot quite committed to the idea that the pursuit of scientific knowledge was a central means by which God's power and truth could be understood. Further, the monastery was located in Brno, the provincial capital of Moravia where there were several scientific societies fostering a community of amateur naturalists, associations not uncommon in the nineteenth century, and prior to Mendel's arrival the monastery had been mandated to teach mathematics and religion at the Brno Philosophical Institute. Thus, Mendel landed in a very supportive environment that encouraged the pursuit of his interest in science and mathematics.

Consistent with this dual mandate of religious and secular enlightenment, the local priest noted that Mendel was "very diligent in the study of the sciences but much less fitted for work as a parish priest." His scientific acumen was appreciated and he was reassigned to teach in a Gymnasium in the region and to continue with his scientific inquires. In support of this role, the abbot arranged for Mendel to go to the University of Vienna. Mendel became an "assistant demonstrator" at the Physical Institute at the university working under the direction of Professor Andreas von Ettingshausen, who was known for his work on the mathematics of combination theory. The exposure to this line of mathematics proved crucial in Mendel's study of the bases of hereditary as it gave him an

---

[4] This section draws extensively on Robin Henig's (2001) history of Mendel and his work.

analytical structure within which to consider the combinatorics of dominant and recessive traits that are the core of his scientific contribution.[5] In addition, Mendel become exposed to prior scientific work on hybridization and to early, emerging work on the cellular basis of biological life. This exposure enabled Mendel to engage in a "Schumpeterian"-like creative recombination of taking the mathematics of combinatorics to the novel application domain of the study of heredity.

There had been an extensive body of work exploring hybridization, including with regard to the common garden pea which became Mendel's experimental platform. However, previous researchers had focused on the qualities of the plants as a whole, a focus compatible with the then dominant "blending inheritance" theory that offspring were a mix of the traits of their parents and that their characteristics would tend to lie intermediate between the qualities of the parent. Mendel, in contrast, focused on individual traits of the plants (height, color, nature of seeds, etc.). This distinct unit of analysis was crucial for Mendel to discern the pattern of recessive and dominant traits. It was this insight of dual inheritance and the qualities of "dominating" and "recessive" that allowed him to make sense of the empirical patterns he observed in his experiments and led to the conceptual break with theories of blended inheritance.

Mendel was a scientist of considerable talent and enormous drive and persistence. However, both the happenstance of his academic influences and the supportive "niche" of his abbey were critical factors in enabling his process of discovery. He approached the problem of hereditary with the knowledge of the mathematics of combinatorics and operated in an organization that valued his scientific pursuits despite its theological underpinnings and mandate. His own life journey of intentional search and discovery, heavily influenced by this path-dependence and the "artificial" selection environment in which he as a scientifically oriented religious figure operated, are nicely illustrative of the theoretical perspective developed here and he himself serves as evocative metaphoric figure for these arguments.

---

[5] Mendel's efforts to apply the mathematics of combinatorics to other domains, such as the compound words that formed common German surnames, proved less valuable, but all these efforts point to the importance of the happenstance of this exposure.

2

Choice, Selection, and Learning

Simon (1976 [1947]) in his introduction to *Administrative Behavior* offers up a provocative equating of processes of deliberate choice and processes of selection. He states the following:

> All behavior involves conscious or unconscious selection of particular actions out of all those which are physically possible to the actor and to those persons over whom he exercises influences and authority. The term "selection" is used here without any implication of a conscious or deliberate process. It refers simply to the fact that, if the individual follows one particular course of action, there are other courses of action that he thereby forgoes. In many cases the selection process consists simply in an established reflex action .... In other cases the selection is itself the product of a complex chain of activities called "planning" and "design" activities .... The words "choice" and "decision" will be used interchangeably in this study to refer to this process. Since these terms as ordinary used carry connotations of self-conscious, deliberate, rational selection, it should be emphasized that as used here they include any process of selection, regardless of whether the above elements are present to any degree.   (Simon, 1976 [1947]: 3–4)

Simon's use of the term "selection" as an overarching construct that includes our conventional notions of choice as well as less deliberative action is useful framing for a broadly structured evolutionary perspective. What is arguably distinct among processes of choice, learning, and what we conventionally think of as selection is the basis of the selection criteria. In the case of rational, or even merely intentionally rational choice, selection is driven by a projection of the future consequences of alternative actions. In contrast, evolutionary selection processes are driven by the contemporaneous relative fitness of alternatives, where in the biological case these "alternatives" are different organisms.[1] Yet a third perspective is that of learning.[2] Here, the preferential attraction to different alternatives is backward looking. That is, actions that are perceived to have been associated with more successful outcomes are more likely to be enacted than those associated with less successful outcomes.[3]

In a similar vein, Dennett (1995) contrasts three archetypes: a Darwinian process of differential selection over phenotypes, or forms; a Skinnerian processes of the reinforcement of behaviors; and what Dennett terms a Popperian process. The Popperian label is inspired by Popper's observation that the capacity of humans to engage in hypothesizing and counterfactuals allows "our hypotheses to die in our stead." That is, in contrast to a Darwinian process where the form survives or die, in a Popperian process the mortality of ideas and beliefs can precede those who carried those ideas and beliefs. A Popperian process requires an actor to have an internal selection criterion that can evaluate alternative actions on the basis of their possible consequences. This "internal selection" criterion need not have a strong correspondence to the true external selection environment in which the actor operates, and the quality of "foresight" can be interpreted as the degree to which there is a correspondence between the current internal selection criteria and the future external selection criteria.

In this regard, a "catholic" view of choice may be characterized as the identification of preferential action over some set of latent

---

[1] While in an evolutionary process selection is based on current measures of fitness, this fitness is the result of a particular prior history of modification of the form and prior selection forces. This prior history creates the "fodder" over which current selection forces operate and in that regard this contemporaneous selection process is quite history-dependent and in that sense is also "backward looking."

[2] In is interesting to note in this context that Thorndike (1899) in motivating his argument for the law of effect, a foundation for work on reinforcement learning, made an analogy to the theory of natural selection.

[3] A process of Bayesian learning, a critical element in rational models of decision-making, generates a similar sort of backward linkage. However, the Bayesian updating of beliefs is then an input to a forward-looking calculation of subsequent payoffs, while in a process of stimulus-response learning there is no forward-looking calculus and only "backward-looking" associations.

opportunities. This is, admittedly, a somewhat awkward linguistic construction, but this awkwardness is intentional so as to avoid connotations that might be evoked by our usual ideal types of choice, reflexive learned behaviors, or selection. At an abstract level, "choice," "learning," and "selection" have some fundamental commonalities. All of these mechanisms take as input an alternative set of some form and privilege a subset of these alternatives to form the basis of action. There are two critical factors on which these mechanisms differ. One that is perhaps more salient but less consequential is the contrast between a deterministic operator associated with choice, particularly with ideas of rational choice where a unique optimum is assumed to be identified, and the probabilistic process by which beliefs map to action in models of learning and the probabilistic way in which relative fitness expresses itself in survival rates in a process of selection. What is a more central difference is the bases of evaluation: pass outcomes (learning), current fitness (selection), and projections of future outcomes (choice).

2.1   Encoding of the Past and Projections of the Future

Whether the evaluation mechanism is future (intentional choice), current (evolutionary), or past (learning), it is important to confront the question of how performance or fitness (future, current, or past) is understood or operationalized. When we think of the problem of firms' strategizing, we take as the criteria the metric of a firm's profits. While conceptually a well-defined construct, as a practical matter it is a measure that is strikingly problematic. Any action the firm, or more specifically any action an actor within the firm, might take has both immediate and longer-term consequences. Further, if we consider the action of an individual or organizational subunit, we face the issue of potential interdependencies among actors and subunits. While one might with some level of confidence anticipate those outcomes relatively near-term and local to the actor, the longer-term consequences of many actions cannot, in general, be anticipated with any level of assurance.

Not only is there the problem of forecasting future states of the world, but firm decision-making is nested in an arbitrarily long multi-stage decision problem in which actions at one time period not only yield immediate outcomes, but also change the state of the system (the firm) as it confronts new states of the world and new decision opportunities. This is not a problem unknown to decision theorists and fits neatly within the framework of dynamic programming. However, while dynamic programming offers a clear solution algorithm to relatively simple problem settings—simple in terms of number of stages of decision-making and number of interdependent actors, such as the two-firm, two-time-period economic models common in the study of firm strategy in industrial organization (Fudenberg and Triole, 1988)—it is a much more limited tool in more naturalistic settings of extended time horizons with decisions that are linked both inter-temporally and spatially. Bellman (1957), a key developer of the techniques of dynamic programming, referred to this as the curse of dimensionality. In the face of the intractability of the underlying problem context, the pragmatic use of intentional rationality entails the use of some form of simplified cognitive representation of a more complex, unknowable payoff surface (Levinthal, 2011).

In considering how an "engineering" of evolutionary dynamics might operate given these challenges, it is useful to consider the line of work in machine learning starting with the pioneering work of Samuels (1959, 1967) on credit assignment, later built on by Holland (1975), as well as more contemporary work on "actor-critique" models (Sutton and Barto, 1998; Singh et al., 2010), in which reinforcement is based on a value function that constitutes a learned reward function. In Samuel's early work on developing machine learning algorithms for playing checkers, the key insight was that using as a reward the final outcome of a win or loss was a very poor basis for learning an effective strategy. Such a reinforcement mechanism does not provide a direct means of identifying the value of interim "stage-setting" moves such as controlling the center of the board. He introduced the notion of credit assignment that was later built upon by Holland (1975) and Sutton and Barto (1998), whereby moves that lead to states that are viewed as valuable would themselves be reinforced.

In a similar fashion, when organizations define milestones and metrics around key success factors, they are constituting an artificial selection environment that guides the cultivation of initiatives within the firm (Levinthal and Warglien, 1999). The virtue of such shaping rewards (Elfwing et al., 2008) is that they may substantially speed up the feedback process relative to the feedback from the environment as to whether a given action or strategy is pushing forward along a promising track. In this manner, the valuation of these interim outcomes can help counter the myopic tendencies of direct reinforcement learning processes (Levinthal and March, 1993).

Similarly, in both operationalizing and conceptualizing the processes of learning, there is the issue of the encoding of outcomes. A central argument in March and Simon (1958), and built on by a large body of subsequent work within the "Carnegie" tradition, is the dichotomous distinction between "success" and "failure."[4] This dividing line between success and failure is not treated as a fixed value or absolute; rather, it is treated as itself adapting to the history of outcomes (Cyert and March, 1963). As more recent scholarship has highlighted, the aspiration level may also take social references as its basis (Greve, 2003). Interestingly from the perspective of the argument developed here a social aspiration level can approximate a conception of an evolutionary selection process. From the perspective of a social referent, actions are viewed as favorable only if they yield outcomes similar to or superior to the firms' reference set. Indeed, if we substitute the word "niche" for "reference set," we come close to a restatement of the basic structure of a selection process.

While the literature on organizational learning has played considerable attention to the question of what factors influence an aspiration level, demarking what constitutes domains of satisficing

---

[4] This distinction builds on Simon's earlier dichotomization of "satisficing" alternatives in his model of choice (Simon, 1955). However, for Simon in his model of bounded rationality, this dichotomy of "satisficing" and "non-satisficing" alternatives is a future-oriented projection regarding the anticipated payoff associated with a given action. In models of learning, this is an interpretation of past outcomes into these discrete categories.

and non-satisficing outcomes, far less attention has been devoted to the challenge of a possible plurality of outcomes. These issues are, however, beginning to rise to the surface (cf. Ethiraj and Levinthal, 2009; Joseph and Gaba, 2014), particularly in the context of the consideration of hybrid organizational forms with dual goals of social impact and profitability (Battilana and Lee, 2014). While the work on hybrid organizations illustrates the challenge of the multiplicity of overarching objectives, another mechanism by which a multiplicity of outcomes may present challenges and opportunities for a learning process is the disaggregation of experience. Consider, for instance, the work on learning from near-failures (March et al., 1991). Airlines not only have crashes, but they also have near-misses. A near-miss can be viewed as a "success" in that there was not a collision, but it can also be interpreted as a failure in that the planes came closer than safety would suggest. Similarly, in Vaughn's (1996) account of the Challenger disaster, for some actors within the organization the frayed O-rings identified on prior landings of the Challenger constituted a failure of the technological system; however, for higher level actors in the organization, the previous safe and timely landing of the ship was sufficient to constitute success.

Thus, while keeping to a dichotomous distinction between success and failure, with the disaggregation of outcomes we shift from a world of "black and white" to a world that consists of different shades of gray—gray at least in a pixilated manner of individual "cells" (i.e. distinct, specific outcomes) of black and white (Levinthal and Rerup, forthcoming). Where an actor sits within an organization, and in turn the criterion they are likely to evoke as to what constitutes success or failure, is likely to vary their interpretation of outcomes.[5] As Lewis (2005) observed, "what you see and hear depends a great deal on where you are standing; it also depends on what sort of person you are." While the image of nested levels of selection was introduced in the introductory chapter from the

---

[5] In this sense, where an actor sits within the organization and the distinct perspective on what constitutes success and failure that that location entails, is akin to the role of a niche in a process of selection.

vantage point of a "Mendelian" intentional designer, the discussion here points to a potential complex ecology of interpretation and selection. The subsequent chapters on selection (Chapter 4), exploration and exploitation (Chapter 5), and punctuated change (Chapter 6) develop these ideas more fully.

In sum, the critical distinction among the processes of choice, selection, and learning is the basis of evaluation—respectively, projected future outcomes, current performance, and the encoding of past performance. Further, as developed in subsequent chapters, selection criteria themselves are subject to change, though typically on a slower time scale, and these changes in selection criteria can have dramatic impact on the subsequent adaptive dynamics.

Exploitation-Exploration and the Softmax Operator

The exploration-exploitation tradeoff is central to evolutionary processes (Holland, 1975). Starting with Holland's pioneering work, the multi-armed bandit problem has been treated as a canonical problem context with which to examine this tradeoff. The "bandit problem" poses a task environment in which an actor is faced with a set of alternatives, each of which may generate a distinct stochastic reward. This simple structure captures core elements of the exploration/exploitation tradeoff as an actor may be preferentially attracted to an alternative for which they have some degree of confidence that this alternative would generate a positive payoff versus choosing a different alternative for which there may be more uncertainty and even lower expected payoffs. Learning in this setting is online (Gavetti and Levinthal, 2000)—information about the value of an alternative can only be generated by direct experience with it. Thus, experimenting with the novel comes at the opportunity cost of not benefiting from the familiar. In the absence of this opportunity cost, there would be not be an exploration-exploitation tradeoff, but rather a problem of search and sampling (cf. DeGroot, 1970). In a pure search problem, there is a direct cost of search or sampling, for instance the cost of surveying a customer or

Continued

Continued

running a laboratory experiment, but not an opportunity cost—search on one option does not preclude searching, or using, other options.

The softmax decision rule was introduced by Luce (1959) to capture experimental evidence as to how actors change their choice in response to stochastic rewards. It has also been adopted as a key component of models of choice in bandit task environments (Holland, 1975; Posen and Levinthal, 2012). The softmax rule characterizes the choice of alternatives as a function of the ratio of beliefs regarding the attractiveness of a focal alternative to the sum of the beliefs of the full set of alternatives evoked. Further, this function takes a parameter, τ, often termed the "temperature" that tunes the odds of selecting the actions perceived to be more favorable. As this term is reduced, the probability of the chosen alternative corresponding to the alternatives perceived to be more favorable increases; conversely, as this term increases there is an increasing degree in randomness in the choice. More formally, the expression is: $p_t(a) = exp(q_t(a)/\tau)/\Sigma\ exp((q_t(i)/\tau))$, where the summation in the denominator is taken over all n alternatives.

Thus, the softmax rule has elements of learning, namely how beliefs about the attractiveness of the various alternatives change with experience with them. Further, per Simon's use of the term "selection" as an overarching label for choice processes, the specific action in which the actor engages in is determined by the relative "fitness" (perceived attractiveness) of the various alternatives. The selection criterion is relative beliefs as to how promising the individual alternatives are and the intensity of the selection process is specified by the parameter that tunes the exponential function of beliefs. Further, the "temperature" term, τ, of the Luce choice model can be interpreted as an indicator of the degree of exploration or exploitation in which an actor engages (Holland, 1975; Sutton and Barto, 1998; Posen and Levinthal, 2012).

As a mechanism by which the competing claims of "exploration" and "exploitation" are navigated, this structure helps us identify three different ways in which phenomena of exploration and exploitation have been interpreted (Posen and Levinthal, 2012). Empirically, one typically treats "exploratory" behavior as corresponding to actions that have not previously been taken (Lavie et al., 2011). However, conceptually, we often think of the balance between exploration and exploitation as a strategy. Exploration and exploitation as a "strategy" corresponds to the τ parameter in the softmax rule. However, how exploratory or exploitive the behavior that results from a given strategy, or τ value, is, is in turn mediated by how skewed or diffuse these beliefs are of the attractiveness of the various alternatives. For example, if an actor has relatively diffuse beliefs, then even a strategy that is somewhat exploitative will generate a fair degree of exploratory (i.e., novel) behavior. By contrast, if beliefs are highly skewed, that same search strategy (τ value) would generate behavior that would appear to be relatively exploitive. Thus, the overall mechanism is best understood as a "triad" of beliefs, strategy, and behavior. As an illustration of the interplay among this triad of beliefs, strategy, and behavior, Posen and Levinthal (2012) show that exogenous shocks to the value of the alternative arms causes beliefs over the attractiveness of the alternative arms to become more diffuse. As a result of these more diffuse beliefs, search, in the form of shifting behavior, occurs endogenously with these shocks without any shift in strategy, τ, of the balance of exploration and exploitation.

3
Path-Dependence

Imprinting effects have long been understood as having important and enduring impacts on organizations, whether that imprinting is the social context at the time of the organization's birth (Stinchcombe, 1965) or particular features of the founding entity (Barron, Burton, and Hannan, 1996; Beckman and Burton, 2008). But imprinting is not a statement of inertia. We are then left with the challenge of understanding not only the possible shadow cast by an organization's initial state, but more generally the constraints and opportunities that its history entails. There are a number of concepts in the management literature that speak in some fashion to this issue. Terms and concepts such as path-dependence, real options, and dynamic capabilities are among the more salient of these. In this chapter, we attempt to provide a careful rendering of these terms and concepts.

Living things are the product of two factors: the characteristics of their initial genetic composition and the developmental processes that follow from that starting point. Our borrowing of ideas, concepts, and imagery from evolutionary dynamics within the management domain tends to privilege the variation and selection processes that determine this initial genetic structure, but pays relatively little attention to developmental processes, which in the biological case entails the unfolding from a single cell organism to a multi-million, billion, or in the case of humans, trillion cell entity.[1]

In this chapter, we consider the issue of the concept of path-dependence and what this property means in the context of the

---

[1] Arguably a similar gap was present in the field of evolutionary biology itself until the 1980s, when the discovery of the homeobox genes, genes critical to the playing out of embryonic development, precipitated a flowering of work on the interplay between development of organisms and evolutionary dynamics—what has become known in the literature by the shorthand of "evo-devo" (Arthur, 2002).

process of organizational evolution and change. Critical to this effort is the deconstruction of this overarching construct into the distinct properties of learning, state-dependence, and development. Finally, we consider the concept of dynamic capabilities that has generated considerable interest in the management domain (Teece et al., 1997; Helfat et al., 2007), engaging in a micro-analytic deconstruction of this rich construct.

Before proceeding with this agenda, it is important to tackle a proverbial "elephant in the room" when it comes to considering an evolutionary account of organizations, and that is the issue of whether there is something analogous to a "gene" in the context of organizations. Given that this work is developing a self-consciously evolutionary account of firm behavior, there is a natural question of what might constitute the "gene" of an organization: the enduring traits over which selection occurs and the basis for transformation of organizational attributes from one "generation" to the next. The construct of gene is a very powerful conceptual anchor for Nelson and Winter's (1982) seminal work on an evolutionary theory of economic change, as the construct of a gene in their work embodies the stable differences in firms' capabilities that is fundamental to their analysis. However, as scholars examined the nature of routine behaviors within organizations, they identified greater fluidity in these behaviors than a stylized image of genes and routines might suggest (Birnholtz et al., 2007; Feldman and Pentland, 2003). Further, the nature of this plasticity does not seem well captured by a notion of change via a chance mutation or a process of recombination.

This apparent conflict between the conceptual apparatus of a genetic basis for organizational behavior and these empirical observations can be reconciled if one recognizes that in their original argumentation Nelson and Winter put forth the construct of routines as both embodying the role of gene, the enduring carrier of the information content of behavior, as well as phenotype, the expressed behavior itself. As Levinthal and Marino (2015) observe, a given genotype might give rise to a wide variety of expressed behaviors as a function of the particular circumstances in which the organism (organization) finds itself. To take a trivial example and to return to Mendel and his peas, a given genetic strand of peas will reach different height, color, and taste as a function of the degree of sunlight and moisture to which they are exposed.

While the distinct construct of phenotype, and its many-to-one relationship with a particular genotype (i.e. a given genotype might result in a fairly wide range of phenotypic forms), allows one to incorporate a high degree of plasticity within a genetic-based argument, there are still considerable corollary, potentially problematic properties with using the construct of gene as a conceptual anchor. In particular, there is the question as to what would constitute a generation within an organization.

For the purpose of this work, no claim is made regarding the genetic basis for organizational behavior. Rather, the weaker, but still sufficient claim for our argument is made of path-dependence. In the language developed in this chapter, the firm's attributes in one period impact the set of accessible states as well as the cost of achieving a given set of attributes. Path-dependence is sufficient to make an evolutionary argument of interest. Some degree of inertia is necessary for selection-based arguments to be of relevance (Hannan and Freeman, 1984; Levinthal, 1991a) and, particularly in the context of strong selection environments, path-dependence is a basis of sufficient sustained heterogeneity among organizations so as to make population-level selection processes of relevance (Levinthal, 1997).

3.1 Deconstructing Path-Dependence

While the general idea of path-dependence has become central to the discourse in strategic management, what this construct entails is typically not clearly articulated and it is often evoked to suggest rather different properties.[2] To be more precise, it is useful to conceptualize an organization as a dynamic system—the organization takes actions in a given time period, experiences a given external context or "environment," and as a joint consequence of these actions and the environment may both realize changes in its

---

[2] This subsection bears significant imprint from conversations with Thorbjørn Knudsen.

attributes and some immediate payoffs. With this structure in mind, we can now delineate three quite distinct forms of path-dependence.

First, there is a process of *learning* in which, as a result of a prior pattern of action-outcome relationships, the propensity to take specific actions when faced with a specific situation may change. It is important to emphasize what this use of the term learning does not imply. First, it is not intended to suggest that the changed propensities regarding what actions are triggered by a given setting lead to superior realized, or even expected, outcomes. Second, the term learning is used here to reflect propensities to engage in specific behaviors, but not a change in the set of possible behaviors. Even as narrowly specified here, learning processes are important and underlie much of the improved performance that organizations experience in a given task setting (Argote, 1999). Of course, superstitious learning is also possible (Lave and March, 1976). Further, as Denrell and March (2001) observe, building on an early insight of Mark Twain (1897), there can be a "hot stove" effect in which inaccurate beliefs persist as one's current beliefs affect the sampling process, so that actions that are viewed as having negative consequences are not sampled and therefore those beliefs are not subsequently corrected.[3]

A second, distinct process is *state-dependence*. What is entailed by this construct is that the set of accessible states may depend on the existing properties of the organization. Dierickx and Cool's (1989) discussion of asset stock accumulation is a form of state-dependence. Per their discussion, for example, a firm's history of advertising efforts will impact its brand name at a given point in time. To help identify the distinct properties of a state-dependent process, consider the simple, highly stylized example of a random walk. At each stage of this "walk," the distribution of the change in the state variable remains constant; however, the likelihood of reaching a particular state at a future time period $t+1$ is very much contingent on the value of the state at a prior time period t. More

---

[3] Twain's (1897) observation was that we should be cautious about over-interpreting experience and offered up the illustration of a cat who jumped up on a hot stove and might have learned from that experience not to jump on any stove, hot or cold, and given the behaviors guided by that belief would never be disabused of its belief.

generally, state-dependence captures the notion that the realized values of critical state variables, such as brand-name or capital stock, depend on the historical and cumulative flow of activity and resources towards the building of these state variables. Returning to the example of a random walk process, what states are achievable at a given time period are a function of the prior history of actions, but the transition probabilities between any two states remain constant over time. Thus, the constraints on what is possible to achieve at a given point in time are determined by the value of the state variable at that time and not by the probability distribution of the transitions that might be experienced.

We reserve the term *development* to refer to a change in form of the entity and operationalize form in this context as a capacity to move though some possible state space, and not merely a change in the state of the system as in the example of a random walk. A simple, and therefore perhaps useful example is to consider how the capacity of a human being to travel a given distance changes markedly over the aging process, from the near immobility of an infant to the modest range of a short-legged and easily tired toddler, to the expansive range of a mature youth or young adult, and finally again to a limited range of an infirm elderly individual. This differential range of possible movement in a period of time need not have any relationship to the starting point of a given journey, i.e. the issue of state-dependence.

What might, in turn, underlie the process of development? As the example of human aging suggests, certain changes in the phenotype are trigged by a temporal clock in the organism's genetic structure. Processes of cell division, decay, and alternative structures are triggered by chemical signals reflecting both genetic imprinting and autocatalytic processes within the body. More germane to the problem of organizations is the fact that actions, investments in technical capabilities, or initiatives that restructure the organization and change underlying processes may not only change the state of the system, such as the issue of stocks and flows in the case of state-dependence, but may change the capacity for the organization to act and realize distinct outcomes in the future. In that sense, the development of an organizational capability is transformative.

Not only is it useful to distinguish development from other processes underlying the dynamics of organizational and population-level change, it is also useful to free the term from some of the conceptual "baggage" with which it is often associated. Development is not deterministic, either in its timing or its outcomes, and may reflect important sensitivity to the environmental setting in which it takes place. As noted with Mendel's peas, the development process is very much a function of the conditions, and in particular the resource environment to which an entity is exposed—sunlight and water in Mendel's context and forces such as macroeconomic and technological change in an organizational setting. The stylized, and in many respects quasi-deterministic stage-like conceptions of development offered in the past in the management literature (Greiner, 1972; Kimberly and Miles, 1981), may have added to our collective blinders to these dynamics. In the field of evolutionary biology, the linkage and dual role of evolution and development is an important and active line of inquiry (Pigliucci, 2001; Hall et al., 2003). While social entities clearly have distinct dynamics from biological ones, at the same time an evolutionary perspective on organizational populations would seem to be importantly lacking without some attention to the role of development and its place in these broader evolutionary dynamics.

3.2 Development and Selection

Further, recognizing the presence of developmental processes highlights issues regarding the timing and intensity of selection pressures (Levinthal and Posen, 2007). Selection operates on the temporal unfolding of the phenotypic expression of a given form, as well as to the differential technical performance of mature expressions of the form. An evolutionary perspective is fundamentally related to the temporal unfolding of processes of organizational and industry change. This temporal unfolding is critical to our understanding of how selection processes play out, a property that has arguably been underappreciated. We tend to think of selection as operating on some population of entities with fixed traits; however, in view of the significant degree of possible phenotypic change over an entity's lifetime, the timing and intensity of selection with respect to the developmental clock is critically important (Levinthal and Posen, 2007). Consider this issue in the context of a start-up enterprise. Its current "form," whether expressed in terms of personnel, technology, or products, is generally merely a faint shadow of its ultimate possibilities. At the same time, lacking much in the way of financial and non-financial resources, a startup is quite vulnerable to the vagaries of the selection environment in which it operates and, in particular, its set of current and latent funders and product market competitors. Thus, recognizing the joint consequence of development and the genotype/phenotype distinction opens up a wide range of important issues.

Consider, for instance, the contrast between r- and K-strategists that Brittain and Freeman (1980) highlighted. Firms of the "r type" are able to be rapidly mobilized and to enter into a market or niche in response to a perceived opportunity, whereas "K type" firms are slow to mobilize but are capable of achieving high levels of efficiency. Put in developmental terms, r-strategists reach something approaching their adult form rapidly and early on in their life histories, while K-strategists have a more extended "birthing" period and "childhood." The survivability of these alternative forms then importantly depends on the timing and intensity of selection pressures, as well as whatever buffer stocks firms may be endowed with that may attenuate selection pressures (Levinthal, 1991b; Barron et al., 1994).

The timing of the relative plasticity of the organization also has important implications for the long-run consequences of the particular historical sequence of environments that an organization experiences. This issue is readily seen in the context of human development. For instance, a child exposed to multiple languages becomes bilingual, whereas an adult having the same exposure is more likely merely to become confused. It is reasonable to suspect that analogous phenomena are present in the organizational context. Exposure to varied environments early on in an organization's life history might engender a robustness and flexibility, while if this exposure does not first occur until a later life point when relatively entrenched patterns of behavior have developed, it may pose a threat to the organization's life chances (Barnett, 2008).

Further, development not only leads to relatively fixed and rigid forms, but developmental processes may also generate modules and building blocks that provide opportunities for further change processes. Modules and sub-structures, the outgrowth of prior developmental efforts, themselves change what might comprise the set of accessible states. Indeed, the combinatoric possibilities of the modularization of practices and technologies have been recognized as a critical factor in the speed with which organizations and social systems more broadly may access alternative forms (Baldwin and Clark, 2000; Schilling, 2000; Ethiraj and Levinthal, 2004).

In this spirit, while the label path-dependence generally connotes the constraints and the imprinting of past actions, competitive positions, and beliefs—the chains of the past as it were—it is important to also consider the dual of this standard "backward-looking" engagement with the notion of path-dependence. If existing attributes of the organization are to provide a basis for advantage in a future period, then there must be some linkages between the future state of the firm and this prior state. In the absence of such a linkage, these subsequent states would be accessible by any number of other firms and fail to provide a basis of competitive advantage. The concept of organizational routines (Nelson and Winter, 1982) is a powerful illustration of this duality: routines are simultaneously enabling and constraining—facilitating the organizations' effective engagement in some range of behaviors, while creating rigidity and inertia relative to other possibilities (Leonard-Barton, 1992).

3.3 Real Options

The notion of real options has been a central framework by which prior behavior is linked to future possibilities via a rational choice approach (McGrath, 1997; Bowman and Moskowitz, 2001; Trigeorgis and Reuer, 2017). Initial investments in a so-called "stage 1" both lead to some degree of updating about the value of subsequent investment, but also lower the cost or make feasible the possibility of subsequent investment to realize an opportunity. As an illustration of the later property, perhaps some initial investments constitute the acquisition of some property rights over an asset, such as an oil tract, a movie screenplay, or patent. In other settings, the cost of realizing an opportunity is lowered as a result of time-compression costs (Dierickx and Cool, 1989; Hawk et al., 2013) such that by making antecedent investments in various capabilities subsequent states can be achieved with less cost than if they were approached in a more discrete manner. More generally, the notion of privileged access to future states is central to the idea of "real options."

Less appreciated in the discussion of real options is the question of firm differences at the onset of what is taken to be the "stage 1" investment.[4] If firms are effectively homogeneous a priori, with no propriety knowledge of the prospects of a given alternative and no propriety access to an investment in any particular set of alternatives, then the purchase of a real option would be akin to buying a lottery ticket. Essentially firms would be like a homogeneous consumer, each free to bet on any set of numbers in a lottery that they wish. Thus, real options are important not only in how an initial investment opens up a distinctive set of opportunities, but also in how a firm's existing position and capabilities change the value of alternative options. As an illustration of such considerations, Wu et al. (2014) show that established firms may "bet" on technologies that appear inherently less promising if their existing capabilities are complementary to those technologies.

The current set of actions, capabilities, and market position, constrain the achievable set of actions, capabilities, and market positions that may be obtained in subsequent periods and influence the payoffs as to what might constitute more or less desired positions. The past casts a shadow on the set of future possibilities. While evolutionary accounts highlight the constraints of past actions and investments, forward-looking rational choice accounts highlight

---

[4] A separate issue that has generally been neglected is the interim evaluation of these staged investments. That challenge is taken up in section 4.2 of the following chapter.

the flip-side of the constraints of path-dependence: how investments "today" may enable opportunities "tomorrow." This idea is core to the notion of real options in which initial stage-setting investments provide privileged access to future opportunities. In the absence of path-dependence, there would be no need to consider real options— a contemporaneous, myopic view would suffice in such a setting. Thus, whether one takes a "glass half empty," backward-looking approach that highlights the constraints that path-dependence imposes or the "glass half full," forward-looking approach of real options that highlights the enabling role of current actions, path-dependence is central to the consideration of either perspective.

3.4 Dynamic Capabilities

As noted, a fundamental conceptual challenge is to characterize the accessibility of different states. Consider the following simple abstraction. Take a firm at time period t. What are the accessible states that can be realized in a subsequent time period?[5] Posing this question forces one to confront what one considers the relevant unit of analysis. If we consider the corporation from the perspective of the ownership of a set of assets, then period-to-period change can be quite dramatic. However, while the reshuffling of ownership structures may have dramatic effects on the composition of the firm, it need not have any direct or immediate effect on the underlying operating units (Penrose, 1959).

The construct of dynamic capabilities (Teece et al., 1997; Helfat et al., 2007) has been put forth as a way to understand firms' differential capacity to access alternative states. It is useful to deconstruct this rich and rather complex set of ideas. Such a deconstruction

---

[5] Of course, the answer to this question importantly hinges on what constitutes the time span of a "period" with the set of accessible states increasing with this magnitude. For the current purposes, it is useful to have in mind some "medium" time span such as a fiscal quarter or calendar year. Very short time spans, say a day, are not terribly interesting as future possibilities are largely defined by current activities. Over very long time spans, there is a large set of accessible states. However, over long time spans, the question of what insights might guide organizations to different regions of this vast state space arguably starts to take primacy over the question of accessibility of these states.

suggests five distinct facets of this construct. First, if we consider a firm as being characterized by some vector of attributes at time t, $(a_{1,t}, a_{2,t}, a_{3,t}, \ldots a_{N,t})$, then the issue of accessible states is simply what constitutes the set $(a_{1,t+1}, a_{2,t+1}, a_{3,t+1}, \ldots a_{N',t+1})$ of possible realized states.[6]

A conceptually distinct issue, which generally is not incorporated in discussions of dynamic capabilities but might profitably be so, is the concept of robustness. Robustness does not entail the transformation of attributes, but rather speaks to the range of states of nature over which a given set of attributes maintain their value.[7] Formally, robustness can be characterized as follows. Let us consider the value of a firm's attributes at period t by the function $V(a_{1,t}, a_{2,t}, a_{3,t}, \ldots a_{N,t}|s_t)$. The issue of robustness can then be represented by the difference between this valuation and the value of the function at an alternate state of nature, s_{t+1}, realized at a future period $t+1$: thus, $V(a_{1,t}, a_{2,t}, a_{3,t}, \ldots a_{N,t}|s_t) - V(a_{1,t}, a_{2,t}, a_{3,t}, \ldots a_{N,t}|s_{t+1})$. In follow-up writings on the notion of dynamic capability, Teece (2007) placed a greater emphasis on the role of dynamic capabilities in "shaping" future states. Analytically, this can be expressed by a function that maps the firm's current vector of attributes and the current state of nature to a future state of nature: $s_{t+1} = g(a_{1,t}, a_{2,t}, a_{3,t}, \ldots a_{N,t}|s_t)$.

Related to the prior discussion of the contrast between the ownership of assets and a shift in the underlying operating capabilities of the firm is the question of the cost of achieving a given set of attributes. As Barney (1986) and others writing within the resource view of the firm have noted, it is important to consider strategic factor markets, where the term strategic factors references those attributes that underlie differential firm performance and thereby stand in contrast to commodity inputs that would not have such a link to performance. Formally, this is a function of the form: $c\,(a_{1,t+1}, a_{2,t+1}, a_{3,t+1}, \ldots a_{N',t+1}|a_{1,t}, a_{2,t}, a_{3,t}, \ldots a_{N,t})$. Issues of privileged access to resources and capabilities posed in the prior discussion of real

---

[6] Note that as indicated in this formulation both the values of the attributes may change as well as the number and type of attributes.

[7] In this regard, it is important to distinguish between "states" of the firm, which are characterized here by a vector of "attributes" and states of the world, often referred to in formal models in decision theory and economics as "states of nature" (Savage, 1954). Further, it is important to note that "states of nature" should be understood as including the actions, capabilities, and competitive positions of other firms.

options and of time compression diseconomies (Dierickx and Cool, 1989; Hawk et al., 2013) underlie the nature of this function.

Lastly, there is an issue that generally is not posed in the discussion of dynamic capabilities and that is the question of assessing, a priori, the value of accessible states. Beliefs about the value of future possible states clearly influence the firm's investments and actions in the present and, as a consequence, which future states will be realized. One can consider these beliefs as simply reflecting a probability distribution over possible future states of the world: $p(s)$. However, there is another fundamental consideration and that is the nature of the valuation function itself: $V(a_{1,t+1}, a_{2,t+1}, a_{3,t+1} \ldots a_{N',t+1} | s_{t+1})$. Winter (*1987*) refers to this as the "imputation problem." While trivial to state such a function, its properties are terribly complex. As a consequence of some degree of path-dependence, the value of a given set of attributes in period $t+1$ depends not just on the properties of the state of nature in period s_{t+1}, but also possibly on the value of all future states of nature. Path-dependence makes the firm's strategic problem a multi-stage game. Furthermore, as noted earlier, this is an unbounded problem that suffers from what Bellman (1961) termed the "curse of dimensionality." As a consequence, forward-looking strategic choices generally require the invoking of some form of a valuation heuristic. This issue is woven into our consideration of selection processes in Chapter 4.

3.4.1 Dynamic Capabilities: Nouns, Verbs, and Firms

While the initial work on dynamic capabilities (Teece et al., 1997) had its intellectual antecedents in the resource view of the firm, subsequently a more process-oriented perspective on the question emerged (Eisenhardt and Martin, 2000). Conceptually, it is helpful to contrast the idea of a dynamic capability as a "noun," some specific capability that facilitates one of the five properties noted above, versus a "verb," a consideration of processes associated with organizational change. With regard to the noun-like sensibility, absorptive capacity (Cohen and Levinthal, 1989 and 1990) would be a prime candidate example of this sort of attribute, as the presence of absorptive capacity not only impacts the transformation of the firm's technical capabilities in conjunction with changing technological possibilities, but also influences the firm's ability to make judgments regarding the prospects of such changing possibilities (Cohen and Levinthal, 1994).

However, dynamic capabilities may also be usefully understood as a process, as "verbs"—processes that impact the likelihood and value of changes in the firm's strategy and resources. It is the latter focus that is developed here. Processes of organizational learning, as well as processes of variation and selection, impact organizational adaptation. Organizations may vary in the efficacy with which they carry out such processes. It is a useful shorthand to reference these different bundles of processes as a "capability." Furthermore, there are some attributes, such as alliance capabilities (Kale and Singh, 2007), that entail a mixture of "nouns" and "verbs." A firm may have developed a dedicated function within its corporate development office for identifying and managing alliances and that office, in turn, is likely to have developed a set of processes, rules, and routines for being effective in this task.

An important limitation of both "noun" and "verb" approaches to the question of dynamic capabilities to date is that they tend to look at these attributes in isolation. However, organizations are complex adaptive systems. It is, in general, problematic to identify a particular attribute of such a system and to suggest its implication for the behavior of the overall system. Rapid learning at one level may substitute or negate learning processes at another level (Levinthal and March, 1993). For instance, March (1991) shows how rapid learning at the level of individual actors may reduce the rate of learning for the organization as a whole.

In a similar spirit, it is important to note that the value of a firm's efficacy at engaging in recombinations is a function of the "fodder" over which these recombinations can occur. This line of argument is taken up by Levinthal and Marino (2015). They develop a model of hierarchical learning inside organizations with the goal of examining the interplay among the different elements underlying the broader construct of dynamic capabilities. In particular, they point to the adaptive tradeoff of the flexibility entailed by the plasticity of individual routines, with the effect of more plastic routines in mitigating the effectiveness of selection processes within the organization. Organizations with a rich and diverse "fodder" of fixed underlying practices may prove more adaptive than if those individual practices were themselves subject to change and less reliably subject to selection and replication processes.

3.5 Summary

Path-dependence is a critical, but also arguably under-theorized construct, as it has become a carrier for a number of distinct ideas and processes. This chapter attempts to provide some useful unpacking of this rich concept. The intertemporal linkages that both constrain and enable an organization are central to its adaptive properties. The most narrow expression of path-dependence is the process of state-dependence—having a particular asset stock at one point in time impacts the distribution of asset stocks that can be reached at a subsequent period, even if the mechanisms associated with and the capacity for organizational change itself have not changed. Development, how an organizational form unfolds over time, can change those dynamics.

A considerable literature has sprung up around the idea of "dynamic capabilities." This broad idea is broken down into five distinct facets: accessibility of organizational states, robustness of organizations to change in the state of nature, capacity to influence future states of "nature," cost of accessing future sets of attributes, the capacity to value the merit of having a set of organizational attributes in a future period. However, the discourse on dynamic capabilities tends to treat capabilities as isolated attributes and not to view the organization as a complex adaptive system. As a complex adaptive system, it is problematic to assign value to an attribute in isolation, such as the rate of learning of a particular element within this system. This view of the organization as an aggregate and a consideration of how the various processes within the organization and external to it affect the organization's adaptive dynamics are central to the perspective developed here and in particular to our understanding of the exploration/exploitation tradeoff as discussed in Chapter 5.

Path-Dependence, Spandrels, and Equifinality

A central "engine" of management theorizing is some form of contingency theory. The basic structure of such arguments is that, associated with a given environment E, there is a preferred organizational form F and if the environment were to shift to some E', there would generally be a new preferred form F'. Similarly, the primary analytic device of neoclassical economics is comparative statics (Samuelson, 1947), where one identifies the qualitative movement in decision variables with the shift in some exogenous (to the decision-maker) parameter.

Path-dependence suggests that there is not a universal best or appropriate response to a given environmental change, but rather the response to such changes will in general depend on the existing state of the organization. Such dependency will be present when some form of internal contingency or interdependency within the organization is present. Wright (1933) introduced these ideas in evolutionary biology with the framework of "fitness landscapes." If the mapping between a string of genotypes to the fitness of the associated phenotype is a many-to-one relationship, then whether a "flip" of a single genotype is fitness-enhancing may depend on attributes of the other $n-1$ genes. As a consequence of such interdependence, the fitness landscape will have multiple local peaks. Kauffman and Levins (1987) provided an analytical formulation of Wright's ideas, a formulation that was then applied to the phenomena of organizational evolution by Levinthal (1997) and developed further by a number of scholars (see Baumann, Schmidt, and Stieglitz, 2019 for a review).

Among the implications of a landscape lens of the process of evolutionary dynamics is the possibility of equifinality, that qualitatively different forms may yield similar performance payoff or fitness. Such a perspective argues against the emergence of a single ideal type form.

Another implication of multiple peaks and possible non-convergence to some unique dominating form is the limitation to transferring apparent wisdom or preferred practice from one "form" to another. The transfer of practices is itself a widely adopted management practice and a mainstay

Continued

Continued

of many consulting engagements. However, recognizing interdependencies cautions against the presence of universal best practices. Affirmatively, what this perspective suggests is the power of transfers, or imitation, that are to a large degree "context-preserving." A ready example of context-preserving transfers of practices are transfers within a multi-unit corporation, with franchise systems being a salient illustration (Bradach, 1997; Sorenson and Sørensen, 2001; Winter et al., 2012). Within the same organization, even if only a single practice is transferred, a large broader assemblage is often shared in common. A stronger form of "context preservation" is when the replication is not at the practice level but with respect to the overall phenotype, or form. In this spirit, Winter and Szulanski (2001) highlight the phrase and sensibility of Intel's managerial practice with respect to transferring semiconductor manufacturing processes of "copying exact" the full ensemble of practices and processes.

The issue of preserving context raises the challenge of distinguishing between "hitch-hiker" genes, traits that are correlated with critical attributes but are not themselves important, and traits or practices that may play an important role, but whose role may not be self-evident. Lansing's (1987) examination of the Balinese water temples is an extraordinary illustration of the potential pathologies from a lack of discernment between artifacts or "spandrels" (Gould and Lewontin, 1979) and key functional features. To the social engineers trying to introduce the Green Revolution to the rice farmers of Bali, the various practices associated with the broad system of water temples were a gratuitous anachronism. However, as Lansing demonstrates, the temples and the associated rites were in fact central coordination mechanisms preserving the fertility of the agricultural system. The well-intended intervention to rationalize and modernize this system considerably damaged this fertility, damage ultimately undone by the resumption of the historical practices.

Path-dependence also entails "inefficient histories" (March and Olsen, 1984). One form of "inefficient histories" is highlighted in work on network externalities (David, 1985; Arthur, 1989) which demonstrates that a population of actors may converge to a less preferred technological standard. Gould and Lewontin's (1979) discussion of the Spandrels of San Marco and Gould's (1980) later "tale" of the panda's thumb illustrate a different sort of "inefficient history." Gould argues that one of the key empirical traces of evolutionary processes is the frequent inefficiency of the "design." Spandrels are a by-product of the engineering and architectural problem of constructing vaulted domed cathedrals, making use of the space leftover from the supporting arches (Gould and Lewontin, 1979). Similarly, while the panda is unique among Ursidae (bears) in having an opposed digit, a thumb as it were, the panda's thumb was an outgrowth and repurposing of an extended wrist bone and is not in fact an opposed digit (Gould, 1980).

Thus, while a Darwinian process is often reduced to the syllogism of the survival of the fittest, "fit" is not simply a function of the environment or niche in which an organization operates. First, there is a consideration of "internal" fit—the degree to which the various properties of the entity are compatible and possibly even reinforcing (Siggelkow, 2001). Second, there is the issue of external fit that links the current array of organizational attributes to measures of performance. The two challenges are related. Changes to enhance external fitness are predicated on the current array of attributes, which themselves are a legacy of prior efforts to enhance fitness that were in turn influenced by the existing attributes at the time of those prior changes. This joint process of navigating internal and external fitness acerbates the challenge of management interventions or social engineering of broader systems more generally in discerning among features that might be irrelevant to the intervention (spandrels and hitchhiking genes), those that prove beneficial, and those that could be damaging.

4
Selection

Ideas, business plans, off-sites, and design efforts do not themselves directly receive rewards from the market. Organizations do. While there is a large nuanced literature on the theory of firm, the term "theory of the firm" has taken on very different connotations within the economics literature (Coase, 1937; Williamson, 1975; Gibbons and Roberts, 2013) and behavioral traditions (Cyert and March, 1963). In the economics literature, the motivating question under this rubric is the question of the appropriate scope of the firm's boundaries. For Cyert and March (1963), the motivating agenda was an empirically grounded account of firm behavior. The ensuing "Carnegie School" has emphasized the role of search, problem-solving, and feedback learning processes (Gavetti et al., 2007). Within the evolutionary economics tradition (Nelson and Winter, 1982), the firm is the central carrier of the enduring basis of capability differences and the object over which the selection force of competitive dynamics operates.

Building on this evolutionary perspective, a basic overarching fact about organizations is that firms receive profits and losses, while individuals generally only receive rewards as mediated by an organization's accounting system and incentive structure. In that sense, a firm can be considered to be a credit assignment mechanism (Holland, 1975). Understanding the nature of these processes is a fundamental challenge for management scholars. In this chapter, we consider three basic challenges in this regard: the problem of diversity of selection criteria, the challenge of the timing of selection relative to developmental processes, and the issue of units of aggregation and selection.

One might object to this line of argument in the context of for-profit enterprises as the "for-profit" objective would nominally seem to obviate the need to consider multiple selection criteria. However, even putting aside the issue of divergent stakeholder interests, even in the context of a for-profit enterprise a superordinate goal of maximizing the net present value of the enterprise still leaves open the issue of what might constitute the most meaningful and reliable metrics associated with progress towards this end-goal. The property that strategic initiatives have implications across time and/or "space" (other initiatives within the organization), corresponds to Andrews's (1971) classic contrast between what is considered "strategic" and what is "tactical." Reflecting these properties of temporal and spatial linkages, in this chapter we link the consideration of selection criteria to the issue of the timing of developmental processes and the units of aggregation which form the bases of evaluation. Further, we recognize that the environment, or contexts, in which the organization operates is itself an object of selection, which in turn influences the feedback processes the organization experiences.

4.1 Challenge of Diversity of Selection Criteria

It is important to contrast the diversity of underlying elements—people, ideas, routines—and the diversity of selection criteria. While we tend to privilege the former sort of diversity as critical to processes of innovation and change, there is a relative neglect of the role of the diversity of selection criteria—the diversity of perspectives as to what constitutes useful endeavors for an organization, the alternative means by which an agreed upon goal might be best achieved and the associated implications of these potentially diverse perspectives for an organization's resource allocation processes. Underlying this difficulty of organizations sustaining a diversity of selection criteria is the tendency for resources to be allocated by a hierarchical authority structure within an organization.

Our discussions of innovation and change tend to highlight the role of variety. However, variety alone is clearly not sufficient for innovation. To take Kanter's (1988) imagery of "letting a thousand flowers bloom," such diversity in blooming will not be of consequence if the organization only has one type of "lawnmower," or less metaphorically, one type of screening criteria.[1] While obviously a caricature, the point is that experiments must be complemented by sufficient variety in the feedback mechanisms and selection criteria that inform the internal selection process within an organization (Adner and Levinthal, 2008).[2] Innovation within organizations requires resources; therefore, sustaining diversity requires ongoing resource commitments to a diverse set of emergent efforts.

We explore this question of heterogeneity of selection criteria in a number of respects. First, feedback, whether through learning at the level of an individual actor or via differential selection among a set of entities, is dependent on context. Therefore, it is important to consider the heterogeneous settings to which an organization is, or latently is, exposed. Second, a critical role of organizations is to mediate between aggregate outcomes, profit and loss, and payoffs to individual actors and acts. As a result, it is important to consider in detail the organization as an artificial selection environment (Levinthal and Warglien, 1999) or credit assignment mechanism (Holland, 1975). A critical issue in this mediation of external outcomes or payoffs and the distribution of rewards and feedback to the set of actors and subunits within the organization is the degree to which diversity of selection criteria are present. Diversity can be mitigated by a high degree of centralization of resource allocation as it can be difficult for a single actor to be of "multiple minds" regarding alternatives. However, diversity can also be mitigated by a high degree of socialization and convergent thinking among a set of nominally independent actors (Van Maanen, 1973; Levine and Moreland, 1991).

---

[1] Ironically, Kanter's (1988) phrase, in turn, was presumably at least indirectly inspired by Mao's (1957) famous encouragement to Chinese dissidents to come forth and "let a hundred flowers blossom." Consistent with the argument here regarding the importance of not only initial variety but subsequent selection processes, many of those dissidents who did come forth subsequently faced punishment by the state.

[2] A different mechanism is the role of slack (March and Simon, 1958) or a single screening criterion that is noisily applied (Knudsen and Levinthal, 2007) or imperfectly implemented (Puranam, 2018).

Learning processes are feedback driven. As a result, the particular context in which one operates critically influences the feedback received. Christensen's (1997) work on the disk-drive industry is usefully interpreted in this light. One can take a bundle of performance characteristics regarding cost, processing capabilities, weight, and power consumption and get very different responses in terms of perceived value depending upon which customer constituency one asks. The desktop-user community responded with a shrug of their collective shoulders when offered drives that were smaller and lighter, while the emerging community of laptop producers responded with enthusiasm for such possibilities.

The fact that firms and the products they produce compete in heterogeneous demand environments is an issue that has been of long-standing interest to marketing researchers. However, marketing research tends to suffer the opposite problem of a neglect of "supply side" considerations. This tradition offers methods and techniques to identify heterogeneity of demand, techniques of conjoint modeling and the like; however, this work tends to operate with an implicit assumption of enormous plasticity in the range of what the firm is capable of producing. For instance, the marketing challenge is to understand the appropriate degree of bitterness of a beer, and perhaps what the desired images are to be associated with a product, but there is no question of brewing, of how one might actually produce the beer with the desired attributes.

From a learning and adaptation perspective, heterogeneity in demand context not only says something about identifying desired positioning, but also about what sort of capabilities might emerge as a consequence of the path-dependent development of those capabilities in particular contexts. These ideas are expanded upon both in Chapter 5 where the diversity in selection criteria among actors is argued to be critical in understanding the contrast between exploration and exploitation and in Chapter 6 in the discussion of punctuated change, where it is argued that critical junctures in the evolution of a technology are its shifts to a new application domain (Basalla, 1988; Levinthal, 1998) and similarly how shifts in an organization's artificial selection environment are critical catalysts to organizational change.

4.2   Challenge of Timing of Selection

A different set of considerations revolves around the timing of the selection process relative to the unfolding of any given initiative. Selection is inherently myopic (Levinthal and Posen, 2007). Evaluation of fitness, whether a conscious choice by an organizational actor or external to the firm in the form of product market competition or financial evaluation, is based on the current instantiation of a project or entire organization. Thus, the interplay between the developmental trajectory of an object of selection and the timing and intensity of selection is central to how selection processes will ultimately play out.[3] A salient managerial expression of this tension is the pragmatic playing out of "real options," as well as the development and funding journey of new ventures. These challenges may involve "false negatives" as often lamented, situations in which the near-term feedback is not positive but in fact the unfolding developmental process would lead to an attractive outcome. However, organizations also face the challenge of "false positives" in which early positive signals are not terribly indicative of longer-run prospects. The potential for false negatives should temper enthusiasm for a focus on "early wins"; indeed, Levinthal and March (1993) argue that feedback-driven learning processes can be an important source of myopia. Navigating between these dual challenges of false negatives and false positive is an important organizational challenge (Sah and Stiglitz, 1988; Christensen and Knudsen, 2010; Csaszar, 2013). Indeed, Guler (2018) finds that the effective capability to evaluative incipient ventures is associated with substantially higher returns for venture capital firms.

The link between actions and outcomes occurs on varying time scales. Some actions, such as dynamic pricing for a web retailer, will have immediate observable consequences. However, even such immediate tactical acts may have longer-run consequences on subsequent period sales and potentially even a brand's reputational

---

[3] One might argue that selection forces can operate regarding beliefs or indications of this developmental trajectory; however, the critical property remains that those attributes that inform these interim evaluations need to be visible in some fashion.

capital. Immediate evaluation (selection) of the shift in pricing can only reflect the near-term outcome of a shift in near-term sales. For many initiatives of interest from a strategic perspective, near-term outcomes are a mere shadow of their ultimate payoff. The difficult challenge in devising selection processes is developing temporally proximate indicators that are suggestive of these ultimate payoffs.

In this regard, a striking observation when one looks at the literature on organizational learning is the extent to which this work has examined learning issues in, essentially, selection-free environments. Formal models of organizational learning tend to have the structure of seeding a population of organizations with diverse learning strategies or organizational structures and then observing the variance in performance within the population after some large number of learning trials. However, these nominally process-oriented modeling efforts tend to ignore the path to these performance asymptotes. Imagine that learning does not take place in the benign petri dish of a simulation model, but in a competitive environment in which survival until the end of the period of observation cannot be taken for granted. What then are the implications for the desirability of alternative learning strategies?

First, once learning dynamics are placed in a context of selection pressures, the meaning of what is a high-performing learning strategy becomes non-trivial. Is a good strategy one that generates high expected performance conditional on survival? This is implicitly the criteria of the business press, which tends to extol the virtues of dramatic gambles that paid off well. Alternatively, is a good strategy one that leads to a higher probability of survival? A third option, and a criterion that is used in most models of organizational learning, is the average performance of alternative strategies assuming that *all* organizations survive.

A fundamental problem for selection processes is that selection is occurring over a "moving target" (Levinthal and Posen, 2007). Indeed, as is clear from evolutionary arguments, selection can only be "intelligent" if there is a high degree of stability over what is being selected. However, in the innovation context, it is inevitable and quite appropriate that selection processes are enacted even when development processes are far from complete.[4] Firms need to make interim judgments as to whether to continue to commit resources to a technology or product development effort and often cannot afford to wait for its full fruition or failure. Similarly, capital markets, particularly markets for venture capital, need to make interim evaluations as to whether a given concern is worthy of further resources.

Development paths are subject to more discerning intermediate selection, that is selection prior to the full realization of their potential that is indicative of this ultimate potential, to the extent that the correlation in the performance of development efforts across time is relatively high. To the extent that early success is suggestive of ultimate success, then intermediate selection can operate effectively. Development approaches, however, are likely to vary in their degree of correlation across time. Levinthal and Posen (2007) contrast development efforts in which initial efforts focus on one facet of the overall development effort, which they term the technical development sub-problem, with efforts in which the full business system of technology, manufacturing, and marketing is jointly searched. Exploring sub-problems has the virtue that it leads to rapid early performance gains and therefore is more likely to survive early screening efforts. However, such a search strategy that initially attempts to optimize a particular subsystem will tend to lead to lower correlation in performance across time than an integrated development effort. Thus, while the focused strategy leads to higher survival from early screening efforts, that early filtering process is less aligned with the ultimate selection criterion of the performance of an integrated system. As a result, integrated search strategies are shown to lead to higher average performance *conditional* on survival, even though the average performance under this search strategy in the absence of selection is inferior. Work illustrating the power of modularity tends to ignore these selection and survival considerations.

---

[4] Indeed, one might argue in the context of many organizational initiatives that there is a priori no fixed end-state, but rather these initiatives continue until some future termination or redirection decision.

A further implication of this argument is that introducing survival concerns turns on its head the now established view of managing the dynamics of exploration and exploitation. The standard result from search models is that in early stages one should engage in exploration so as to learn more about the set of possible actions and then, after some knowledge has developed, to engage in more exploitative behavior. However, again, these analyses do not concern themselves with survival. Young, small, vulnerable firms often have an acute survival problem. They need to exploit whatever modicum of wisdom they have about the world if they are to survive. Exploration is arguably for richer, more established firms; indeed, this idea is suggested by the notion of slack search (March and Simon, 1958; Cyert and March, 1963). With slack search, more innovative, exploratory efforts are prompted by performance results in excess of aspiration levels.

A context in which the issue of intermediate selection tends to be both quite important and under-attended to is the use of real options to justify and guide projects and resource allocation. There has been much enthusiasm among academics and practitioners for the tool of real options as a solution to the problem of how firms should manage their uncertain futures, particularly with regard to technological uncertainty (McGrath, 1997; Amran and Kulatilaka, 1999; Trigeorgis and Reuer, 2017). However, as Adner and Levinthal (2004) argue, real options are not quite the panacea that its proponents tend to suggest. The real options argument as applied to problems of strategic management has the following basic structure: the world is uncertain, therefore the firm should make lots of modest-sized "bets" and, as future states are revealed, the firm should exercise those options that now appear attractive, having positioned itself to do so as a result of its earlier investments. One of the basic concerns that Adner and Levinthal (2004) pose is how is the firm to know in this metaphoric "stage 2" which investments are attractive to strike or not. Unlike financial options, for which observation of current pricing in financial markets suffices, real options on technology provide no such clarity.

Indeed, the typical early-stage innovative effort results in a partial failure, or put more optimistically, a partial success. A typical scenario is as follows. Deadlines for technical hurdles are not quite met, but some substantial progress is made. Potential users have not reacted with unabashed enthusiasm for the product, but it appears some modification of the feature set may result in a product with considerable appeal. If this is the modal outcome, what is the implication for managerial action and subsequent resource commitments? In the same spirit, critical to the logic of real options that enhances the value of initial "bets" on risky technologies is that exit and the termination of initiatives is a real possibility. However, analogous to Popper's arguments regarding hypothesis testing that we can only prove hypotheses false, but can never prove them to be true: an innovative effort cannot in general demonstrate the impossibility of future success (Adner and Levinthal, 2004). Rather, one observes a failure of the current embodiment of the technology to meet certain technical standards or satisfy the needs of a particular set of consumers. Such failure does not rule out the possibility that future incarnations of the technology might meet such standards, perhaps by pursuing somewhat different approaches; or, alternatively that the firm might be able to identify a different user community that would respond more positively to the current technology. This issue of a potential never-ending journey of search manifests itself as well in the context of the discussion of lean start-ups in which entrepreneurs are encouraged to "pivot" their way to success (Blank, 2003; Ries, 2011), but seemingly little attention is paid to the possibility that an innovative effort might best be aborted in its entirety.

To preserve the analytical logic of real options, a firm would have to put tight boundaries around the scope of an innovative effort, boundaries concerning technical approaches, markets to which the product is to be sold into, and perhaps temporal boundaries (Adner and Levinthal, 2004). However, imposing such boundaries has enormous potential costs as they deprive the firm from taking advantage of the unanticipated discoveries of possibilities that is common in innovative efforts. Thus, real options may certainly be applicable to situations of well-defined risk, where there is uncertainty over known possible states of the world, but are deeply problematic in the face of more ambiguous environments.

4.2.1 Online versus Offline Evaluation

A central building block of the behavioral theory of the firm is the notion of bounded rationality (Simon, 1955).[5] In contrast to the optimizing agent of neoclassical economics, Simon offered the satisficing decision-maker. Furthermore, the set of alternative actions are not presumed to be laid out in their entirety ex ante, but must be discovered or searched. This facet of the behavioral theory of the firm (March and Simon, 1958; Cyert and March, 1963) is by now well established. However, another critical facet of bounded rationality has been largely ignored in this tradition, and that is how alternatives, once identified, are to be evaluated.

Two points are focal in Simon's argument regarding bounded rationality. One is that only a subset of the entire space of alternatives is considered in a given choice setting. Furthermore, decision-makers may be confronted with a sequential unfolding of these possible alternatives, even among the limited set considered. Second, he postulated that these alternatives are evaluated by a simple discrete value function that distinguishes between satisfactory and unsatisfactory outcomes. In this sense, Simon substituted for the usual objective function of economic theory an additional constraint of what constitutes a feasible solution to the choice problem. What is less salient, though considered in the original discussion, is how actors are to evaluate the proposed solutions or alternatives. How do we know whether the various feasibility constraints are satisfied or not? Simon notes that there may be uncertainty as to whether a particular alternative may yield a state of nature that is in the satisfactory set or not, but suggests that this indeterminacy may be resolved by identifying a new alternative that does not suffer this risk.

Yet, this discussion points to an important lacuna in this early work and subsequent development of this line of inquiry. While ideas of search are central in behavioral theories of the firm, the mechanisms by which these alternatives are evaluated are less

---

[5] This subsection draws from Gavetti and Levinthal (2000) and Levinthal (2002).

clearly developed. Typical models of adaptive search have the following characteristics. Some space of possible alternatives is sampled. The realization from this "draw" is then compared either with the current status quo action or in other cases with an aspiration level. When the space of alternatives constitutes attributes such as prices, the model does not seem to require any elaboration. However, consider other possible spaces of alternatives, such as the space of possible new production technologies for a factory or the space of possible spouses.

When presented with a new alternative from one of these sorts of "spaces," how is one to recognize a satisfactory solution when one is confronted with one? Quick inspection of a possible spouse or a production plan may reveal certain proposed alternatives to be unsatisfactory, and some basic constraints or criteria may be revealed to be violated. However, the satisfaction of other constraints may not be so self-evident. How will the workforce respond to the production process? How reliable will the process prove? Similarly, will this proposed spouse prove to be an enjoyable companion upon repeated dining experiences, and will they prove reasonably tolerant of your array of annoying habits? The evaluation of proposed alternatives is a relatively undeveloped facet of the behavioral theory of the firm.

To provide some structure with which to consider such issues, it is useful to distinguish between two sorts of evaluation mechanism: the distinction between "online" and "offline" evaluation (Gavetti and Levinthal, 2000). Online evaluation refers to those settings in which evaluation can only take place by actual trial of the proposed alternative, whereas offline evaluation indicates the ability to assess value in the absence of such a trial. As with many dichotomies, this one is both informative and misleading.

The distinction is clearly important. Some possibilities are evaluated by thinking, by imaging possible futures should that alternative (spouse, production process, etc.) be adopted. Sometimes this thinking is supported with various tools of analytical reasoning, such as spreadsheets and yellow-pads. However, the dichotomy is also quite misleading. There is an enormous gray area between these two poles and most evaluation processes occur somewhere in this intermediate zone. New production processes need not require shutting down the firm's entire operations and substituting the proposed process. One plant may serve as a test, while the prior technology is exploited in the remaining plants. In cases of more incremental changes, only a single line or shift of the production process may be sufficient to serve as an experiential basis on which to evaluate the proposal. The pilot plant operates at a smaller scale than the ultimate substantiation of the alternative would imply, but again it allows a detailed examination of feasibility at lower cost and lower risk than full adoption.

In other cases, an "artificial" environment is created in order to evaluate a proposed alternative that does not introduce the risk associated with a full commitment to a specific initiative. A particular type of artificial environment, wind tunnels to test the performance of new aircraft, offers some additional insights regarding the boundaries of on- and offline evaluation. Wind tunnels allow engineers to test loft and drag in a variety of conditions for a prototype of a possible airframe. However, wind-tunnels have substitute modes of evaluation. One, of course, is to engage in the enormous financial commitment of the full development of a working aircraft and the run the human risk posed to a pilot by the testing of such a craft. The other route is cognitive: to build computer models that simulate the performance of proposed designs. As knowledge of the underlying material and aeronautical engineering improves, offline evaluation can substitute for more online forms of evaluation. But note that this is really a matter of degree. The computer simulation in some form creates its own kind of experience base. It is simply a lower-cost artificial world than ones that involve building physical artifacts. Among the interesting properties of recent advances in 3-D printing is that this technology radically reduces the cost of bridging the digital world of possible forms and the physical world of particular forms.

A different sort of experience is the experience of others (March et al., 1991; Miner and Hanuschild, 1995). This sort of experience has the virtue that trial does not require the disruption of one's own activities; and, furthermore, that the set of alternatives that can be explored at a given time are potentially quite vast. Its weakness lies, of course, in the inferential difficulties that such a process poses.

How much does one learn by watching a potential romantic partner with another what they would be like as a potential partner? Or, perhaps less daunting, how much does some other plant's experience tell one about their own firm's likely success with a new production technology? We are probably more comfortable with generalizing from vicarious learning in the latter case, but that may in part stem from the fact that more of us have experience with the former context than in being plant managers and are more keenly aware of the idiosyncratic features of such relationships than of production processes.

In some sense, the issue of on- or offline search becomes less a categorical distinction than factors that influence the cost, risk, and possibly accuracy of the evaluation process. Online search often entails a particular sort of cost, that of the opportunity cost of not making use of established options. It is this opportunity cost that underlies the tension in the oft-cited exploration/exploitation trade-off. In turn, the degree to which current operations are disrupted by the need to evaluate a proposed alternative influences how painful that trade-off is.

Neighborhood search (March and Simon, 1958), in this regard, has a distinct virtue as it provides an effective, though not necessarily optimal, balance for the need to explore in an online manner alternative bases of action, while at the same time, neighborhood search exploits current wisdom about the world by means of the local nature of the search process. The need for this balance between exploration and exploitation depends centrally on whether the evaluation process of proposed alternatives is on- or offline. Thus, the wisdom of a particular sampling strategy is intimately connected to the possible form of evaluation of those samples. Many of our discussions of search processes have suffered by not sufficiently disentangling these two features of search processes (Knudsen and Levinthal, 2007).

4.3 Units of Aggregation

Behavioral arguments stemming from the Carnegie School treat organizations as being feedback driven (Levitt and March, 1988): actions that are associated with positive outcomes tend to be reinforced and more likely to be invoked in the future in similar circumstances, while those associated with negative outcomes are less likely to be invoked in the future in similar circumstances. But this correspondence between action and outcome is a function of the level of aggregation at which both actions and outcomes are experienced, a consideration that has not generally been highlighted or extensively developed in the literature. Boundaries and the scope of activities have important consequences for both processes of feedback and adaptive dynamics, as well as for the playing out of selection processes.

As a consequence of the fact that selection processes are mediated by the organization, the scope of the enterprise impacts how selection processes play out. Perhaps the most fundamental fact about business organizations is that they comprise an aggregate unit by which a vast set of underlying activities is allocated payoffs by an economy. As a consequence, a critical organizational property is how the firm mediates between the aggregate outcomes experienced at the organizational level and the underlying initiatives and activities within the firm. The fundamental engine of adaptive learning is feedback and the linkage between a focal action and observed outcomes (Levitt and March, 1988). This linkage is more strongly felt and more apparent to the extent that actions and outcomes are local to one another and are more proximate in "space" or time (Levinthal and March, 1993). As a consequence, structures imposing or facilitating the patterning of relationships among actors affect the development of capabilities in a variety of ways.

The logic of the diversified firm is that there are non-trivial interdependencies among elements of the enterprise. These interdependencies, in turn, raise a challenge for resource allocation. A long-standing argument in the business strategy literature has pointed to the power of de-averaging, both with respect to understanding the firm's cost drivers and the value of customers, as a mechanism by which to create a more effective basis for resource allocation than that offered by more aggregate units of analysis that might mask key elements of heterogeneity (Ghemawat, 2002). Similarly, work in corporate finance has argued that diversified firms tend to engage in inefficient resource allocation due to incentive conflicts among operating units (Stein, 2003). However, these efforts at "de-averaging" make the implicit assumption that the individual divisions and projects that serve as the elemental units in the resource allocation process are independent of one another—a property that runs counter to the fundamental logic of a diversified firm.

In this regard, it is useful to return to Simon's classic work on the architecture of complexity (Simon, 1962). Natural and artificially designed systems tend to be nearly decomposable, meaning that interdependencies are not scattered and widely diffused but tend to be focused and localized. Treating subsystems as independent may be a useful simplification or fiction, but it is important that strategists recognize that it is a fiction. Treating the system as a whole is not cognitively possible or practical—indeed Simon suggests that whether or not systems are in fact nearly decomposable, we need to perceive them as such in order to understand them. But, again, while not fully engaging with the full array of interdependences, it is important to maintain some level of mindfulness of their existence and the recognition that any strict decompositions are a possibly convenient fiction of a more complex reality of some degree of interconnectedness even among subsystems that are treated as being disjoint.

Organizational structures and budgeting systems serve as category structures and decompositions. The key levers of corporate strategy are essentially ways of bracketing the interdependence among subunits and averaging and de-averaging these sets of activities. For instance, consider GE under Reginald Jones who, with the help of McKinsey, developed the substructures of strategic business units (Joseph and Ocasio, 2012). Jones felt that the existing "coarse-grained" structuring of GE's activities did not allow him to really understand the underlying businesses and to allocate capital intelligently among them. In response to this, he developed the more fine-grained structure of strategic business units to address that challenge. Once we recognize that any given structural arrangement will inevitably imperfectly capture the true structure of interdependencies, it suggests a healthy skepticism regarding any extant structure.

These arguments suggest that we should not be focused so much on the identification of a Platonian ideal structure, but rather to recognize the imperfections of any given structure and maintain some openness to the possible value of the re-bracketing of activities. The pattern of relatively frequent reorganization is often viewed as a pathology of organizational life and an indication of management failure or fickleness. While there certainly may be instances of failure to conceive of an appropriate design or executive "fickleness" and perhaps the need for new executives to provide their own imprimatur on the organizational structure, there may be a functional role for such changes as well.[6]

De-averaging helps to surface potentially important new investment opportunities that may lie buried within a larger budgetary unit. Indeed, the encouragement to "split off" units addressing new, emerging technologies, is the primary normative suggestion of Christensen (1997) in his work on how established firms may effectively confront "disruptive" technological change. De-averaging can also facilitate efforts to identify inefficiencies within the organization and support efforts at achieving a superior cost structure. This is a central premise of efforts at benchmarking in which a specific business process is decontextualized from the broader business system and the performance of this specific, isolated process is examined and contrasted with similar processes elsewhere in the focal firm or in other enterprises.

The primary benefit of averaging and more coarse-grained structures is to link within a common budgetary unit activities that have a high degree of interdependence. These activities in a more fine-grained structure, with specific administrative and/or

---

[6] The notion of "fickleness" suggested here differs from the idea of "efficiency fickle" put forth by Nickerson and Zenger (2002). Their argument suggests that the ideal organizational form lies intermediate between any pure form, such as functional or product-oriented structures. The suggestion here is that there is no ideal form, and one form merely makes different compromises and tradeoffs than another. In this spirit, Ethiraj and Levinthal (2009) show that shifting over time among a set of simplified goals, where the articulated goal at any point in time is only a subset of the full set of payoff determinants, facilitates adaptive learning relative to having a fixed goal structure, even one that contains the full set of performance dimensions.

accounting decompositions, would create externalities with the impact of choices made within one unit effecting other units of the firm. Per the issue of the importance of treating these issues from a dynamic perspective, it may be that at a certain point it is useful to operate at a relatively coarse-grain level of aggregation in order to allow managers to realize latent scope economies and to learn to manage these interdependences. Having identified these linkages and begun to develop routines and procedures to regularize their coordination, the "scales" may shift and the firm may be better served by then de-averaging these business initiatives to enhance incentives and clarify the best use of the firm's capital.

In sum, the corporation at its core is fundamentally a decomposition of economic activity within the broader economic system. Within its own boundaries, the firm must make further decompositions, or de-averaging, facing tradeoffs regarding the need for coordination, the provision of powerful incentives, and the appropriate allocation of capital. Work in business strategy and corporate finance has, rightly, highlighted the returns to de-averaging with respect to the capital allocation process. At the same time, we must not lose sight of the role of the firm in coordinating economic activity and managing interdependencies among facets of the firm. Absent strong interdependencies, the market and the price system serve as an effective means of incentive provision, coordination, and resource allocation (Baldwin, 2007). As nearly, not fully, decomposable systems, any bracketing of activity will be incomplete or, put differently, not true to the underlying structure of interrelationships. Thus, efforts at specifying appropriate budgetary units must inevitably trade-off incentive intensity and an allocation of capital that more or less strongly corresponds to the underlying structure of business opportunities with realizing the latent benefits of the coordination and linkages among those opportunities.

4.3.1 Organizations and Multi-Level Selection

In addition to being linked spatially, another fundamental fact is that organizations have a hierarchical structure. This hierarchy opens up the possibility of selection at multiple levels. In particular, while selection forces operate on the organization as a whole, the organization itself operates to select the various elements within its boundaries. The term artificial selection environment within the organization has been introduced here to contrast this intra-firm selection force with the "natural" selection environment of market forces. Some projects are curtailed while others are scaled up. Some products are taken to global scope and other products are supplemented. This process of internal selection may well itself be driven by stable operating routines. For instance, Burgelman (1994) observed how fabrication facilities were allocated to different product lines within Intel based on the profit margins the firm experienced on these products. In contrast, the R & D resources were allocated based on the firm's conception of its strategy, which at the time was that it was primarily a "memory company" and that memory components were key technology drivers for the firm. As a result, the firm shifted its production capacity to logic chips, where the profit margins were high, and at the same time continued to devote the bulk of its R & D resources to memory products. Thus, the firm internalized the external selection pressures with regard to production capacity, but with respect to its R & D activity the internal selection environment was loosely coupled to the external environment.

The management literature is replete with tales that illustrate this tension between how initiatives are valued by the organization versus their valuation in some facet of the external environment. The prototypical saga is one of a highly motivated manager (perhaps in a functional role of technologist or marketer) who identifies a promising new initiative for the organization that is subsequently evaluated by their superior. This evaluation may be based on the superior's sense of the external market and the possible payoff to the initiative; alternatively, the evaluation may be premised on the superior's interpretation of the fit between the proposal and their understanding of the firm's strategy.

Consider the feedback processes and selection criteria implied by this process. One basis of evaluation is an untested belief about the market. Such beliefs will persist by the failure to test them (Weick, 1979; Denrell and March, 2001), unless proven to the contrary via vicarious learning from others. The other selection criterion corresponds to fitness with respect to the organization's ongoing policies and, more broadly, its conception of itself (Prahalad and Bettis, 1986). Such a selection criterion is not likely to introduce novelty or act as a source of change for an organization.

Thus, underlying this difficulty of organizations sustaining a diversity of selection criteria is the tendency for resources to be allocated by a singular authority structure within an organization. While a large organization may have sufficient resources to make multiple "bets," those individuals who control resource allocation decisions are unlikely to be of multiple minds. Further, while there may well be considerable diversity of opinion within the organization, there is typically a dominant political coalition (March, 1962) and the perspective of this ruling group will likely drive the resource allocation decisions.

Contrast this characterization to a population of organizations. Even if individual organizations make a singular "bet" with regard to a given opportunity, there may be tremendous diversity across the population of organizations. While there may be some pressure to conform to the perspective of other, respected organizations, individual organizations may receive highly differentiated feedback from their environment and this distinct feedback may lead them to different views of the same business opportunity. Indeed, the motivation of entrepreneurs to leave their prior organization often stems as much from their inability to convince their prior firm to pursue an opportunity that they feel has tremendous promise as it is associated with an incentive to appropriate for themselves the prospective returns associated with the pursuit of that opportunity (Klepper and Thompson, 2010).

Conceptually, a single firm could engage in selective intervention, using Williamson's (1985) terminology, and replicate the virtues of a population of independent organizations. However, as Freeland and Zuckerman (2018: 157) point out, Williamson recognizes that "because higher-level executives always retain fiat rights, they face the constant temptation to use them (and the information gleaned from monitoring mechanisms) strategically and opportunistically, especially vis-à-vis lower-level employees." One way to think about this challenge of a commitment to delegating decision rights is to consider it a problem in "sequential rationality" (Selton, 1975).[7] The corporate office will, in all likelihood, have a point of view about the appropriate direction for the firm and the relative promise of individual initiatives. When faced with a given funding decision, it cannot commit to "throw away" its belief structure or to not act on it.

In contrast, committing to some form of structural decentralization or budget autonomy can act to constrain the central actors from imposing their perspective. In the limit, the formation of a new, distinct organization, freed from any authority structure from the corporate office, is a structural solution to this challenge. Alternatively, it may be possible to design commitment devices that restrict the impulses that make selective intervention problematic from the perspective of sequential rationality. Within an organization, one mechanism is to abdicate budgetary authority. This is often seen on a small scale when a corporation allows a modest percentage of a subunit's operating budget to be used at the subunits' discretion. 3M, and more recently Google, have received attention for instituting such a role at the level of individual managers, who are free to spend a portion of their time pursuing initiatives that they perceive to be valuable (Iyer and Davenport, 2008). The limitation of such an approach is that successful initiatives may not be financially self-sufficient and, as a result, ultimately require supplemental funding. One is then back in the position of having to convince some central authority of the merits of the particular initiative, albeit this evaluation would then occur with the initiative having proceeded with some level of development and therefore would constitute less of an abstract pitch, a glimmer on a white-board, and there would be a greater substantiation of the idea. Thus, the inherent hierarchy of organizations

---

[7] Selten (1975) developed the concept of sequential rationality as a refinement of Nash Equilibria. The critical distinction is that Selten lays out an extensive form treatment of strategic interaction that considers a player's decision at each point in the game tree. Strategies that may be consistent with a Nash Equilibrium that treats actors' overall strategies may not be sequentially rational—when confronted with a choice situation in the playing out of the game, the actor may not find it in their interest to carry out the action associated with the Nash Equilibrium.

(Michels, 1915) constrains the variety that a single organization, independent of its size, can sustain.[8]

4.4 Selection and Shaping of External Landscapes

The imagery of a Mendelian designer of contexts has been put forth up to this point with the focus on the analysis of the firm's internal landscape—the roles, structures, goals, incentives, screening criteria— that managers might set forth within the organization. However, organizations and their Mendelian executives can also influence the context in which the firm operates. There are two basic mechanisms by which such influence can occur. One, which could be viewed as a "selection" effect, is the choice of the contexts in which the organization operates—what are the markets, network of relationships, and so on in which the organization engages. The second mechanism can be thought of as a "treatment" effect. How might the organization influence its environment, whether through direct mechanisms such as lobbying regulatory authorities or somewhat indirectly by acting to catalyze some processes of collective action.

This "selection" into particular markets and market niches influences the feedback that the firm receives and the incentives that it perceives. What markets should the firm serve? What activities should be performed within the firm and what sorts of external linkages should the firm make? These choices provide managerial discretion over the evolutionary path that the firm's capability set takes. A firm's capabilities and market position emerge, are refined, or decay as a result of, or an absence of, product market activity. Therefore, the particular submarkets a firm serves will engender a distinctive, though not necessarily unique, set of capabilities. These capabilities do not follow directly from current operations. However, the incentives the firm has to make various investments

[8] Puranam (2018) offers an interesting counter-point to the loss of variety as a by-product of hierarchy arguing that to the extent hierarchy entails control and information loss, hierarchy will facilitate less centrally directed search and choice processes as a result of this loss of operational control.

and the political forces internal to the firm that may influence such decisions are not independent of its current product market activities.

The selection of the market context in which to operate is a higher-level form of adaptation in contrast to the possibly adaptive responses to the feedback from a given context. This contrast is somewhat akin to the distinction Argyris and Schon (1974) make between first-order and second-order learning processes. The impact on capabilities of serving particular markets is analogous to a first-order learning process. While not automatic, first-order learning processes are a fairly direct outcome of existing structures. By establishing a new set of linkages, whether by choice of a new submarket to serve, a new set of customer relations, or a new internal organizational structure, management sets in motion a new direction for the development of the firm's capabilities and its competitive position more generally. Prescient managers look ahead and anticipate such feedback effects when making decisions about what industries or emerging subfields to enter and which clients may help further the firm's development. Thus, in making a choice about what markets to serve, a firm is making a bet on a co-evolutionary process. The firm is, or should be, not only concerned with its current capability to compete within that domain, but also with how participating in that particular industry or subfield will affect the firm's future capabilities.

Perhaps the most basic attribute of the markets and customers served that will impact the development of the firm's capabilities is their growth rate. Is the firm serving customers and market segments that are growing rapidly, thereby providing a basis for not only significant growth in sales but likely opportunities for cost savings and greater efficiency as well as incentives for innovation (Klepper, 1996)? In addition, leading-edge customers may expose the firm to advances in technology and product offerings (Von Hippel, 1988). The role suggested here of leading-edge customers is similar to Porter's (1990) discussion of demand factors associated with industry performance across nations. Porter (1990) points to two critical attributes of home country demand. One is timing: does the home country tend to be early or late in its demand for a particular class of new products or services? The other is the level of sophistication and the degree to which customers are demanding in their quality requirements. These factors influence the speed and direction with which organizations proceed along their evolutionary trajectories.

4.4.1 Shaping

Gavetti et al. (2017) make an important conceptual distinction between efforts at "search," finding a more or less favorable location on some existing competitive landscape, and "shaping"—taking actions that change some of the properties of the landscape itself. Three different forms of "shaping" are considered here. First, firms are a node in broader technological and economic systems and the value that adheres to any set of firm attributes needs to be understood from this larger systems level perspective. A basic way in which such considerations manifest themselves is the presence of complementarities. For instance, a faster microprocessor may not have much value if the overall speed of computation is constrained by the capacity of the serial bus (Ethiraj, 2007). Work on ecosystems highlights that such interdependencies may be present in aspects of value creation beyond the physical product itself (Adner, 2012). Awareness of these interdependencies informs the preferred locus of innovative efforts (Ethiraj, 2007) and the architectural challenges of linking and inducing the necessary complements so as to support a firm's offerings (Jacobides et al., 2006; Adner, 2012, 2017).

Shaping can also take an important cognitive dimension. An important line of work points to the rule of category definition and legitimation (Wry et al., 2011; Pontikes, 2018). Sociologists have long noted the role of processes of social construction (Berger and Luckmann, 1967) in how societies create meaning and in particular how value is ascribed, whether aesthetics of beauty (Sontag, 2002), genres of music (Phillips, 2011), or food (Rao et al., 2005). These processes of meaning creation do not lie outside the influence of individual organizations. This has been noted in particular in settings of entrepreneurship and market creation, or the "birth" of a new category (Santos and Eisenhardt, 2009; Wry et al., 2011). Even established market categories may be redefined as Carroll and Swaminathan (2000) demonstrate with reference to craft brewers who defined a distinct niche within the broader brewing industry—a niche defined by the nature of their production process, its technical features and its localization. What is critical is not that the niche was defined merely by these technological or market-positioning choices, but that there was an effort to form a collective identity around the new form.

A firm's institutional environment not only influences what might constitute an appropriate set of actions on the firm's part, but the firm's actions may also influence the nature of its institutional context as well (Ahuja et al., 2018). This has been discussed in terms of standard setting (Ranganathan and Rosenkopf, 2014), contesting and supporting the legitimacy of alternative organizational forms (Hsu and Hannan, 2005), organizational practices (Myer and Rowan, 1977; Fligstein, 1985), product market categories (Pontikes, 2018), the design of a firm's ecosystem (Adner, 2012), as well as more traditional considerations pertaining to the role of advertising and brand identity on demand.

One of the challenges in considering the endogeneity of an organization's external environment is the question of what is the degree of plasticity of an organization's context? While an organization may influence its demand environment and institutional setting, there is considerable rigidity and path-dependence in these structures. An organization is not operating on a "blank canvas," but rather a setting of other organizations and possibly entrenched institutional structures. Further, effective influence efforts are often the result of some degree of collective action, identifying shared interest among a set of actors. For instance, legitimating wind power as an alternative form of energy among latent consumers, working with regulators to support its inclusion on the exiting power grid, and addressing technical and environmental challenges is in the collective interest of the broad set of actors interested in developing and pursuing this opportunity (Sine and Lee, 2009). Thus, in assessing what might constitute the "adjacent possible"[9] in

---

[9] Kauffman (2000: 142) characterizes the "adjacent possible" as "all those molecular species that are not members of the actual, but are one reaction step away from the actual."

the space of alternative external contexts, one needs to be mindful of the existing configuration of actors and institutional structures.

4.4.2   What Makes a Good Niche?

One generally considers the question of the environment as a constraint to which the organization must respond. The environment is treated as an "iron cage" that pressures the organization to conform. While there is some truth in that perspective, the environment is also, to some degree, an environment of choice. To the extent that there is such choice, that raises the question of what constitutes a better or worse choice. Three properties of the environment or niche are suggested in this regard: fit, feedback, and malleability.

Fit is the classic consideration of the strategy literature (Andrews, 1971). Strategists are encouraged to map their organization's current strengths and weaknesses into possible market contexts. The literature on diversification adopts a similar sensibility with its emphasis on leveraging current capabilities and resources into additional settings. These are essentially myopic considerations and fall comfortably under the label of "exploitation." These are not trivial considerations and, as with exploitive acts more generally, are central to an organization's near and medium-term survival and performance. However, per the exploration/exploitation tradeoff, choosing contexts to maximize contemporaneous fit is unlikely to enhance long-run survival prospects.

Thus, in addition to these standard considerations of what might constitute a favorable environmental context, there are dynamic considerations of fit. First, what might be more or less promising environmental contexts in the future? When considering this question, it is important to recognize that that promise is not a bet on some exogenously determined "Wheel of Fortune." Rather, a context is promising as a joint property of some of its intrinsic properties and the potential for the shaping of the environment by the organization, possibly in collaboration with other entities. In addition, there is the question of what settings might be more or less generative of future capabilities. Thus, a choice of niches in which to operate is, effectively, a co-evolutionary bet on what opportunities the niche may offer and what trajectory of capabilities and resource the niche may engender.

Thus, organizations themselves are not only complex adaptive system, but they reside in a broader ecology of other organizations and institutions. Distinct niche spaces in this broader ecology provide not only potentially quite divergent selection pressures, but these divergent selection pressures in turn serve as diverse bases of feedback that may influence the adaptive journey undertaken by a particular organization. Further, these niche spaces in which the organizations operate are not inert, nor are the changes they exhibit exogenous to organizations' behaviors. While these influence processes are not determinative and may only be poorly understood by the relevant actors, these external contexts are, to some degree, malleable. The space of the "adjacent possible" niches is to some degree an organization's choice and to some degree of its making.

4.5 Summary

It is argued that a fundamental role of organizations is to mediate between the selection forces in their external context and the specific initiatives and activities within the organization itself. The critical properties of this "mediation" consist of the selection criteria enacted by the organization, the timing and intensity of the selection process that is imposed, and the unit of aggregation at which the selection process operates. Selection is typically not based on some unidimensional criteria such as "fitness" or, in the language of business enterprises, profitability. Even with a shared consensus within the organization of a superordinate goal such as profitability, projecting this objective to particular initiatives situated in a particular temporal and spatial context (i.e. location within the enterprise's broader set of initiatives and substructures) is problematic. Selection inevitably must be made on the basis of various imperfect indicators of broader objectives. The diversity of these selection critera is a facet of the diversity that has been under-appreciated in the literature, which primarily focuses attention on the degree of diversity of underlying initiatives and activities. The enlightened Mendelian executive needs to create structures and processes that recognize the inherent limitations of a singular viewpoint and create structures and processes that moderate their own potentially heavy hand in the internal selection process. Further, the Mendelian executive selects the contexts in which the organization operates, contexts which provide their own distinct feedback and selection pressures, as well as possibly shaping and influencing those contexts.

Selection in Artificial Intelligence: Ex-ante Wisdom and Model-Based Learning

This chapter introduces the premise that an organization can be thought of as a "credit assignment" mechanism that mediates between outcomes experienced between the organization and its environment and the rewards and resources allocated to individuals and initiatives within the organization. Given this perspective, it is worthwhile to consider the body of work in artificial intelligence related to this challenge and, in particular, how different lines of work within artificial intelligence have addressed the problem of how actions and decisions generated by computer algorithms are generated and evaluated.

Since its onset in the early 1960s, there have been two basic approaches in the development of artificial intelligence. In one line of development, there is an assumption that there is some pre-existing knowledge and the challenge is to develop a program that will reliability enact that knowledge. Early efforts within this approach, with Newel and Simon (1972) as the initial contributors, strove to codify the expertise of domain experts through the use of protocol analysis. The decision rules of the experts were codified in a series of "if-then" rules and the broader effort adopted the term "knowledge engineering" (Feigenbaum, 1978).

Continued

Continued

With the development of neural networks (Rumelhart and McClelland, 1986), a very different approach emerged, but an approach that nonetheless still operated on the property that there was clear knowledge of the domain ex ante. This approach became known as "supervised learning." Under this approach, a neural net is trained on a training data set, for instance mammogram images for which clinical assessment had been carried out as to whether the image was associated with the presence of a tumor or not. The algorithm having been trained in this matter is then tested on a hold-out sample to assess its performance.

In important respects, the knowledge engineering approach development by Simon and his students and that of neural nets are vastly different. Knowledge engineering involves making explicit the possibly tacit knowledge of the domain expert and representing that knowledge in an explicit computer code. A neural net does not require or engender any explicit causal model or understanding; rather, it generates a complex set of relationships among characteristics of the stimulus, the mammogram in this example, and the outcome (presence or absence of a tumor in this case). However, there is a known "truth" by which the computer algorithm is judged and hence the label of "supervised learning." In that sense, supervised learning and protocol analysis share the presence of ex-ante expertise. The neural net trained to assess mammograms does not try to peer inside the decision process of medical experts, but it depends on medical experts having created a clinical assessment of each of the images used in the training and assessment process. While the basic structure of neural nets has been long established, their ascendency and prominence awaited complementary changes in the cost and availability of computer power and, even more important, the availability of vast libraries of digital data sets on which these algorithms could be trained and tested.

An alternative approach emerged in parallel from the earliest days of the development of artificial intelligence (Samuel, 1959; Minsky, 1961) that extended classic approaches of operant conditioning (Skinner, 1957) and removed or effectively endogenized the "trainer." Even in task environments that have a finite state representation, such as board games like chess, the number of possible states can be sufficiently large so as to make the exhaustive search for an optimum impractical. Samuel (1959) developed what Minsky (1961: 19) termed an "expectation reinforcement" mechanism. More concretely, moves within the play of the game were reinforced both by an immediate reward that is associated with the move and the valuation placed on the position to which the move lead. However, a critical feature of this approach is that these "valuations" are themselves a learned property, based both on the ultimate outcomes of the game (win, lose, or draw in Samuel's checker-playing program) and, importantly, by the play within a given game (what was the valuation of the new position to which a particular position led). As Denrell et al. (2004) suggest, such an approach allows for a kind of "bootstrapping" of a cognitive model or representation of the problem domain.

Processes of credit assignment, or what some have termed "actor-critique" (Holland et al., 1986) models, have a "Mendelian" quality to them. Assessment is made not merely on the basis of direct trials, but also on the basis of the actor's valuation function. Further, this valuation function itself evolves through experience within the particular context as well as across contexts, with the efficacy of that process being a function of the quality of the categorization schema by which contexts are encoded, a further element in the learning system. The temporal differencing approach developed by Sutton and Barto (1998) has served as the basic "engine" by which such valuation functions are modeled as evolving. Temporal differencing is essentially a behavioral variant of the recursive logic of dynamic programming. In place of the optimal value associated with any state for the subsequent play of the game that is specified in the context of dynamic programing, the actor's current valuation function is substituted and this valuation function itself is reinforced throughout the play of a given game and across the play of multiple, distinct games.

Yet another strand within artificial intelligence is "unsupervised learning." Here there is no "outcome"; rather, the underlying structure of the input data itself is assessed. Variants of this approach have entered the management literature (Hannigan et al., 2019) as a means of distilling

Continued

Continued

from rich text data underlying constructs and relationships. A blending of unsupervised learning and reinforcement learning has developed under the label of "deep reinforcement learning" (Krizhevsky et al., 2012). When the state space of a problem domain becomes quite large and complex, reinforcement learning becomes increasingly inefficient if the process of reinforcement is based on the visitation of specific states. Reinforcement learning in a vast state space benefits from a parallel effort of generalization. An important early exemplar of this dual approach is Tesuaro and Sejnowksi's (1989) program to play backgammon which used unsupervised learning to represent the state space of the game of backgammon and a reinforcement learning process to develop insight about more or less favorable moves within the game given that state space representation. When one moves to even more challenging contexts such as autonomous vehicles, this blending of the representation challenge with the process of reinforcement learning becomes even more critical. Can certain types of slow-moving masses be treated as a category called humans, and, given this category representation, what are reasonable rates of forward movement of the vehicle that both brings it closer to its target destination while keeping the likelihood of intersecting with this slow-moving mass to a minimum. Further, these algorithms are often evaluated in both an "offline" and "online" manner, with an initial training period based on a simulated traffic environment and then the more refined algorithm tested on more naturally occurring settings.

The arch of efforts at machine learning has interesting parallels with our characterization of modes of choice in Chapter 2 and our general identification of a Mendelian "middle ground" between "rational"/divine conception of choice and Darwinian processes of blind variation and selection. The early efforts at knowledge engineering can be interpreted as attempting to capture the wisdom of experts, though in contrast to the usual conception of rational choice the experts were often viewed as having implicit heuristics and much of the effort at knowledge engineering was to bring those implicit heuristics to the surface. While from the perspective of the knowledge engineer and the effort at creating a computer algorithm, the expertise exists a priori. However, the knowledge of the domain expert was a process of both assimilating pre-existing codified knowledge and drawing inferences from considerable direct experience. Credit assignment and actor-critique models are particularly interesting and suggestive from a Mendelian perspective. The valuation function guides the near-term process of reinforcement learning; however, this valuation function itself evolves over longer time intervals. The reinforcement for the valuation function is both a kind of internal validity (did actions driven by the current model and beliefs lead to outcomes that are viewed favorably by the current model?), and the externality validity of feedback from the external environment. Actions are guided by the "artificial selection" of the credit assignment mechanism, but the basis of credit assignment is treated as an informed speculation that itself may change over longer time scales. In that sense, our Mendelian actor serves as a guide to the process of learning and selection, but a guide with modesty about the wisdom of any given manifestation of these guidelines.

5

Exploration and Exploitation

The exploration/exploitation tradeoff captures a fundamental tension in evolutionary systems (Holland, 1975) and has become central in our thinking about the challenge of organizational learning and adaptation (March, 1991). Organizations must make uncertain investments to create the possibility of more promising future, while at the same time they must allocate resources to insure their survival in the face of short-run selection pressures. These are clearly central ideas to our understanding of organizational adaptation.

The fundamental underlying basis of this tension is the opportunity cost associated with exploratory activities, as by engaging in exploration the organization is foregoing the benefits of exploiting its current beliefs and capabilities. If search, or exploration, were purely an offline activity, in the language of the prior chapter on selection, there would be a question of the desired investment in learning and search, but that discussion would not be fundamentally different than other investment activities. It is the fact that exploration is an "online" activity and requires foregoing other activities that are viewed, from the perspective of current beliefs, as being superior that results in this tension between current performance and possible future payoffs. Per the discussion of selection, the intensity of the selection environment in which an organization operates effectively serves as discount rate on the possible future benefits of exploratory behavior, as to reap the fruits of this exploration the organization must survive until that point.

There is a long tradition of work that considers the optimal tradeoff between investing in learning via exploratory behavior and leveraging current beliefs and understanding (Gittins, 1979; Berry and Fristedt, 1985). This "rational exploration" behavior seems at odds with our usual discourse around exploration. Indeed,

March (1991: 71) distinguishes between what he terms "explicit" and "implicit" choices regarding exploration and exploitation noting that:

> organizations make explicit and implicit choices between the two [exploration and exploitation]. The explicit choices are found in calculated decisions about alternative investments and competitive strategies. The implicit choices are buried in many features of organizational forms and customs, for example, in organizational procedures for accumulating and reducing slack, in search rules and practices, in the ways in which targets are set and changed, and in incentive systems.

In much of our discourse around exploration, we are typically referencing what March refers to as these "implicit" choices—not fully calculative tradeoffs of benefits and costs, but a more diffuse sense of benefits or even a less conscious response to norms and values that may animate an actor's behavior. This less fully calculative sensibility as to what constitutes exploration is adopted here. Further, while empirical work typically treats exploration as behavior that deviates from a prior pattern of action (Lavie et al., 2011), conceptually we often speak of exploration as a "strategy." As noted in the appendix to Chapter 2, it is important to consider the full "triad" of beliefs, behavior, and strategy with respect to exploration and exploitation, with the strategy, often modeled as the "temperature" in a softmax operator (Holland, 1975; Posen and Levinthal, 2012), mediating between these beliefs and behaviors. For a given "strategy" regarding search, more or less novel actions will be taken as a function of how tight or diffuse an actor's beliefs are. As a result, if the actor's environment shifts and thereby causes beliefs to become more diffuse, more exploration will result even with a fixed search strategy (Posen and Levinthal, 2012).

Consistent with this distinction between exploration as a behavior and exploration as a strategy, it is useful to take a more actor-centered consideration of the process than our usual more mechanistic images of "long-jumps" or "drawing from urns" provide. These convenient stylized representations of exploratory activities may offer potentially misleading suggestions of actual exploratory processes. To an important degree exploration is not merely the weighing of some individual calculus of risk and reward, but has a social or political aspect of contestation of beliefs and, in many instances, contestation of what constitutes the most critical dimensions of performance. From the perspective of an individual actor, most activities have an exploitative quality in that they are undertaken with the explicit expectation that these actions may achieve meaningful progress on some dimension of performance. In contrast, from the perspective of an observer, these same activities may be perceived as either exploration or exploitation.

In this regard, it is important to distinguish between the perspective of a focal actor engaging in a specific behavior and that of potential "observers"—whether these "observers" be immediate colleagues, one's superiors, or potential investors (Adner and Levinthal, 2008). The wedge between the "actor" and potential others is their possibly divergent beliefs as to not only what constitute more or less valuable actions, but what might constitute more or less valuable outcomes. This divergence may express itself at varying degrees of granularity. It may be that there is shared agreement on a desired superordinate goal (profits) and even the characteristics of an intended product and market; however, there still may be disagreement as to the best way to develop the product or approach a particular market context. We might consider these as tactical differences. Alternatively, there may be higher-order divergence around what might constitute a desired product or market. Indeed, the contestation around what are viewed as exploratory efforts is typically less about operational actions, but more frequently is at the level of the possible merit of new technical functions, new market niches, and the like. In that sense, the problem of search is often less an issue of if we take action "a," will some new product or service "x" be generated; but rather, if "x" occurs, what are our a priori beliefs about the merits of and associated payoffs from "x"?

It is important to contrast this potential divergence in perspective regarding the merits of alternative outcomes from a divergence in goals. For instance, one way in which conflicting interpretation of action emerges in organizations is through different units pursuing their own subgoals. As highlighted in work on modularity (Ethiraj and Levinthal, 2004) and the division of tasks across units (Rivkin and Siggelkow, 2003), the pursuit of actions that enhance performance from the perspective of one operating unit may diminish the performance of a "sister" unit. Imagine, for instance, the impact of the efforts of a product development unit to enhance some technical features on the organization's manufacturing unit. In this regard, the division of labor may beget goal conflict within the organization, even in the absence of any inherent incentive conflict among actors (Ethiraj and Levinthal, 2009; Puranam, 2018).[1] However, while the issue of differing perspective between actor and observer is pronounced in such settings, it is less a divergence regarding what constitutes exploratory behavior versus what constitutes self-interest versus the interest of others. To return to the example of product development versus manufacturing, the industrial engineers working within the manufacturing unit may not doubt that product enhancements are advantageous from the perspective of the product development effort, they simply view them as disruptive from the perspective of their task of operational efficiency and possibly questionable with regard to an overarching goal of firm profitability.

The basis of divergence that is of primary interest here is when actors and observers diverge with respect to their view as to what constitutes the critical metrics by which performance should be judged. In this sense, actors may have distinct cognitive representations of an underlying value function, in contrast to simply differing on what facets of the value function are important to them. This former sort of contestation is more complex and less readily reconciled among actors than a consideration of alternative means to a set of agreed upon ends. For instance, consider the basic n-armed bandit model which has been taken to serve as the canonical representation of the exploration/exploitation tradeoff. A bandit model has a single dimension of performance and therefore no potential

---

[1] This basis for goal conflict lies in contrast with the standard approach in agency theory models where actors are assumed to have some intrinsic basis for conflict, typically stemming from effort aversion on the part of the agent.

contestation as to which constitutes a more or less promising performance gradient.[2] In this setting, the divergence between any set of actors would simply be their view of the likely payoff of the various arms.

In contrast, what is telling in settings where there is, for instance, divergence in beliefs as to what constitute the key elements of functionality in a technology is that a focal actor may be engaging in what they perceive to be exploitive behavior as they "climb" what they take to be the steepest gradient of progress; in contrast, from the observer's perspective, this same actor may be seen as traversing an inferior gradient, and possibly even a negative one. Thus, for the observer, the key distinction between acts perceived as "exploratory" and those perceived as "exploitative" is the extent to which the dimension of performance along which the actor is attempting to progress is recognized and legitimated from the observer's own perspective. In such settings, acts perceived as exploratory are thus arguably more accurately characterized as acts of exploitation by a particular actor or subgroup directed along an alternative performance dimension (Adner and Levinthal, 2008).

5.1 Reconceptualizing Exploration

Our understanding of the exploration/exploitation tradeoff is, in important respects, clouded by our characterization of the activity of exploration itself. [3] As noted, the literature has emphasized the point that exploration is not maximally enhancing to the organization's near-term performance. While this observation is a central property of exploration efforts, it implicitly, and often explicitly, provides an image of exploration as a somewhat random,

---

[2] As characterized in the appendix to Chapter 2, the "bandit problem" poses a task environment in which an actor is faced with a set of alternatives, each of which may generate a distinct stochastic reward. This simple structure captures core elements of the exploration/exploitation tradeoff as an actor may be preferentially attracted to an alternative for which they have some degree of confidence that this alternative would generate a positive payoff versus choosing a different alternative for which there may be more uncertainty and even lower expected payoffs.

[3] This section draws significantly from Adner and Levinthal (2008).

rather undirected search process: drawing from urns, taking "long-jumps," and so on. Such images are arguably misleading. Consider one of the paradigmatic examples of organizational exploration: 3M's fabled policy of allowing scientists to allocate 15 percent of their time and resources according to their individual discretion, a policy made salient in recent years by its adoption by Google/Alphabet. These policies are certainly interesting manifestations of slack search (March and Simon, 1958). However, while there clearly is a sense in which the policy is consonant with the idea of search and discretionary behavior, we need to be careful in how we interpret exactly what such a policy might entail.

The policy provides "slack" in the sense that the individual's efforts are not required to be evaluated according to the performance benchmarks of any of the firm's existing initiatives. However, it also important to note what these individuals are not doing. They are not boating on Lake Superior, nor are they sitting idle in their offices and labs 15 percent of the time waiting for lightening to strike. Rather, these engineers and scientists are working to solve particular puzzles and problems, testing various hunches and hypotheses. A critical feature of these activities is that these initiatives are not undirected; rather, they are "other" directed, where the modifier "other" connotes the notion that the goals and objectives of these discretionary activities need not correspond to the current objectives and strategies of the firm. They are pursuing dimensions of progress that, while possibly not orthogonal to the organization's performance objectives, may not be highly collinear with them. As noted earlier, pursuing divergent objectives or metrics of performance under a common superordinate goal can be understood both at a tactical level of differing views of a preferred path to a shared goal, as in the case of parallel development efforts (Nelson, 1961), or at a more strategic level when the basic dimensions of merit are contested (Kaplan, 2008).

This contestation at the more strategic level regarding dimensions of merit is put in stark relief in Abott's (1884) allegorical tale in which a stranger from "Spaceland" (a world that recognizes three dimensions) attempts to convince an inhabitant of "Flatland" (a world that only recognizes two dimensions) of the existence of a third dimension that he refers to as "height." Discovering that it is impossible to meaningfully discuss the existence of this third dimension using the Flatland's language and metrics, which have no spatial constructs that extend beyond length and width, the Spacelander's only way to convince the Flatlander of the validity of the third dimension is to demonstrate its existence by lifting the Flatlander "up." Upon viewing Flatland from this raised position in which the Flatlander could observe both the two dimensions of the plane as well as witness the new perspective that was offered by the "raised" position, the Flatlander becomes convinced of the existence and potential offered by the new dimension. When the Flatlander returns from his journey, he tries to convince others about the existence of height. However, without the ability to demonstrate its existence by raising them above the plane or to offer a sufficiently compelling argument, he is branded a lunatic and sent off to isolated confinement.

From the perspective of an entrepreneur attempting to achieve progress along new dimensions of performance, colleagues who do not (yet) appreciate the value of the new dimension are Flatlanders. This challenge is present whether we conceive of these potential entrepreneurs as operating on external markets and attempting to elicit resources from venture capitalists and the like or operating in the corporate context and the effort is to elicit resources from upper management. From the perspective of the prospective entrepreneur, their audience is living on the lower-dimensional surface of the officially sanctioned goals and performance objectives of the organization and are sensitive to indicators of progress only on this plane. Entrepreneurs, like Abott's enlightened Flatlander, are engaged in highly directed activity; but, these efforts push them further along a performance dimension that is largely unseen or not highly valued by those around them. In the absence of acceptable validation, their efforts are easily relegated to "blue sky" status and comfortably ignored within their organizational context. If an entrepreneur is to validate these other-directed efforts, they must find a way to validate the new dimension of performance.

In this spirit, managers are often exerted to think "outside of the box," but what constitutes this proverbial box? Generally in the literature, we think of this in terms of the proximity of behavior to current initiatives. A radically distinct behavior is a "long-jump" to a substantially new domain of action. However, even substantially divergent action, if evaluated on the basis of existing performance criteria, results in a certain conservatism. Consider the contrast of Figures 5.1 and 5.2. Figure 5.1 provides the now typical imagery of a rugged landscape. Movement along the domain of action yields a non-monotonic performance payoff. However, Figure 5.1 is conservative in the sense that all the perturbation in performance is constrained to the existing dimension of performance. In contrast, Figure 5.2 indicates how even modest changes in behavior may yield dramatic changes on the new dimension of performance, even if the change in behavior only casts a modest shadow on the existing performance criteria (i.e. the contrast in the movement from A to A′ on the established dimension of performance with the movement along the new performance from the origin to D in Figure 5.2).

This is a departure from the usual distinction between local and distant search. The distance of search is usually measured as the extent of departure from established routines and behavioral

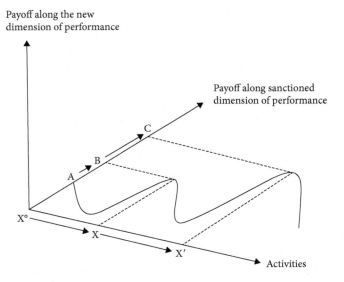

Figure 5.1 Search distance and payoffs along sanctioned dimensions of performance.

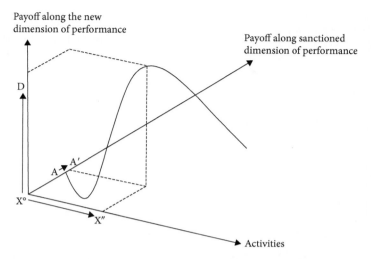

Payoff along the new
dimension of performance

Payoff along sanctioned
dimension of performance

D

A A′

X°

X″

Activities

Figure 5.2 Projections of search along a new performance dimension—casting positive shadows.

patterns. The graphical characterization provided in Figure 5.1 is the tradeoff between the risk of jeopardizing the organization's existing performance position (A) and the promise of finding potentially superior positioning such as B or C that lie at more distant summits that are either a short jump (x) or a long jump (x′) away.

In contrast to this notion of long jumps, the view of exploration developed here need not imply a significant departure from established routines or practices. Rather, it implies a departure from the established metrics of performance or an expansion of the set of measurement dimensions. Since progress along these dimensions is not necessarily correlated, minor departures from routines that show trivial progress along established dimensions might yield significant progress along alternate metrics.

Figure 5.3 illustrates how a moderate departure from existing routines (x″) can simultaneously yield negative progress along the established performance metrics (from A to A′) and positive progress along a new performance dimension (from the origin to D). In this example, progress along the new performance dimension projects a negative shadow along the established dimensions of

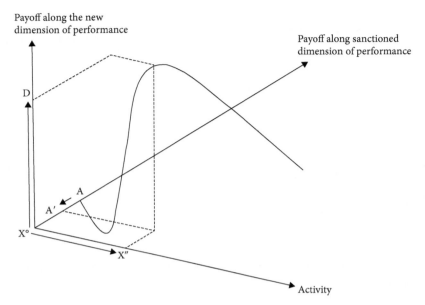

Figure 5.3 Projections of search along a new performance dimension—casting negative shadows.

progress. Christensen's (1997) discussion of disruptive innovation in the hard disk drive industry can be interpreted in this light. Incumbents, who evaluated progress along the legitimized performance dimensions of capacity and speed, did not appreciate the potential of new, smaller disk drive generations—which they themselves had already developed—to contribute to value by progressing along the not (as of yet) legitimized dimensions of portability and energy efficiency.

This "casting of shadows" may have a temporal quality as well. An initiative that seemed irrelevant to Flatlanders may, with the passage of time, come to be viewed as having importance on the existing dimensions of merit. To illustrate this point, consider the basic science goal of measuring the magnetic resonance of the atom and the subsequent application of these insights to the development of Magnetic Resonance Imaging devices. Identifying and measuring the magnetic resonance of the atom was an important question in physics in the 1940s (Bloch et al., 1947) and the basis for awarding of a Nobel Prize to Bloch in 1952. However, it was not until many decades later that the solution to this puzzle in physics cast a "shadow" on the quest for better diagnostic images of soft-tissues, resulting in the development of Magnetic Resonance Imaging (MRI) devises. But again, it is important to note that Bloch and his students were, from their perspective, very much engaged in a goal-directed, problem-solving research of developing precise measurement of electromagnetic radio waves. In evolutionary terms, this can be thought of as an instance of exaptation (Gould and Vrba, 1982), whereby a trait developed for one purpose is adapted to another. This is a line of argument that is developed further in the following chapter on punctuated change.

Established organizations and entrepreneurs confront the problem from opposite directions. On the one side, organizations that seek to foster innovation and entrepreneurship struggle to find ways to encourage managers to pursue new markets and technologies and, as suggested here, new dimensions of performance. Those who take up the call and do pursue progress on new dimensions of performance struggle, in turn, to find ways of legitimizing their efforts, of demonstrating that this new metric is a relevant pursuit in the context of the ultimate pursuit of profitability.

Of course, individuals may perceive possible dimensions of performance that are unlikely to ever have any mapping to any pragmatic "real-world." Poets, dreamers, and budding entrepreneurs may climb "castles in the sky" or "tilt at windmills." An important organizational challenge remains of sorting through initiatives that ultimately pursue novel, but potentially pragmatic dimensions, and those that may only have relevance in the minds of those pursuing a particular performance dimension. How do organizations distinguish between those initiatives that correspond to climbing towards castles in the sky from those that may be unearthing promising new veins of technological progress and product initiatives? An organization's answer to this key question is reflected in its internal resource allocation process and the extent to which this process is designed to support a multiplicity of selection criteria, while still imposing some degree of selection discipline.

5.2 Entrepreneurship and the Legitimation of "Other-Directed" Initiatives

An implication of this distinction between the distance and the dimensionality of progress is that entrepreneurial initiatives must be defined by more than just the novelty of the behavior but also by the novelty by the criterion by which performance is evaluated. Analogous to Knight's (1921) contrast between risk and uncertainty, the variability in outcomes along existing legitimated dimensions of performance is qualitatively different than uncertainty regarding the merit of the performance dimension itself.[4] Strategic initiatives, despite their possible uncertainty, are qualitatively different than "other-directed" initiatives. An initiative's alignment with existing strategic dimensions serves as a potential substitute for direct evidence of its success. The less aligned the initiative, the higher the standard of evidence regarding the likelihood that it achieves its end goals required for its approval—in the absence of legitimacy, hard proof is required. In contrast, the very act of aligning an initiative along existing strategic dimensions serves to legitimate its purpose and, hence, to facilitate a positive selection outcome within the organization.

In the context of corporate entrepreneurship, three logically distinct options seem to be present.

5.2.1 Option 1: Skunk Works

The first option faced by a corporate entrepreneur operating outside of the firm's strategic context is to hide the initiative from the internal selection regime. Such projects rely on the individual commitment of those directly involved with the project for its

---

[4] Knight (1921) distinguished between situations of risk, in which multiple outcomes are possible and in which the probability of these outcomes is quantifiable, with situations of uncertainty in which probabilities are unknowable in advance. From the perspective of the argument developed here, the analog to risk corresponds to the variance in possible outcomes along an existing and agreed upon dimension of performance, whereas the analog to uncertainty corresponds to a lack of clarity or agreement about the appropriate dimensions of performance.

resources and face two distinct challenges. First, because they are necessarily hidden from the larger organization, such efforts face an additional set of challenges in accessing the potentially shared capabilities and resources that would otherwise be available to "legitimate" projects. Second, because incremental success is generally accompanied by increased resource requirements, such projects become increasingly difficult to hide. To the degree that they are hidden from the organizational context, the evaluation of skunk[5] works projects is haphazard, coinciding with their accidental discovery, a need for non-concealable resources, or the unveiling of the completed initiative.

The limitation of such an approach is that successful initiatives may not be financially self-sufficient and, as a result, require additional funding. In such settings, one is then back in the position of having to convince some central authority of the merits of the particular initiative, albeit that evaluation is made over an initiative that is at some further stage of development than it would otherwise be.

5.2.2 Option 2: Retrofit

A second approach is to reframe a non-conforming initiative in a way that fits within the official strategy—that is, to identify ways in which progress along the "other" dimension results in a projection of progress along the legitimated dimensions. Burgelman's (1991) discussion of Intel's venture into Reduced Instruction Set Computing (RISC), a venture that required the allocation of precious development resources away from the legitimated approach of Complex Instruction Set Computing (CISC), is a classic example of retrofit. The RISC effort was justified as a complementary project—one of

---

[5] The term "skunk works" originated in connection with a project at Lockheed Aircraft in 1943 to rapidly create a new fighter jet. The small project team was housed in a remote location and the team adapted the term "Skonk Works" after a Li'l Abner cartoon in reference to an illicit brewery hidden in a forest that was featured in the strip. The term morphed into "skunk works" and has become a label for small, autonomous project teams within a larger organization (Gwyne, 1997).

developing a math co-processor to the core CISC processor—rather than on the basis of the RISC team's true intention—developing a substitute platform for a new core processor. By highlighting the benefits to be gained along the existing performance dimension ("this will make for a more compelling CISC offer"), the RISC team found a way of projecting the progress along their own focal dimension (RISC performance) onto the organization's established performance dimension (CISC performance).

Such subterfuge is required when an initiative is targeting non-legitimated dimensions because, as in the Flatland tale, describing the existence of a new dimension requires a language and a perspective that is unavailable to observers before they are presented with the definitive, visceral proof of the validity of the new perspective. It is only after a Flatlander is confronted with the reality, rather than the promise, of the new dimension that they find the justification to adjust their pre-existing map of the business landscape.

Retrofit may have considerable temporal delay, as an initiative developed on the "sidelines" remains largely sidelined until a propitious moment from the perspective of a policy entrepreneur. Kingdon (1984), applying the Garbage Can framework (Cohen et al., 1972), shows how policy advocates are akin to political entrepreneurs waiting for the alignment of circumstances that allows them to push their agenda to the fore. Kingdon (1984) argues that events, often crises, create "policy windows," brief moments in time during which attention is attached to a particular domain. Successful policy entrepreneurs seize the opportunities and fit their "solutions" to the current perceived "problem" that is galvanizing attention and energy.

Other-directed initiatives face the same challenges in legitimating their claims on resources as did the Spacelander in legitimating his perspective within the confines of Flatland. This is a fundamental challenge for entrepreneurs: how to obtain resource commitments for initiatives that appear "foreign" and at odds with existing business models and logics. While the manner in which this challenge is addressed may be different for de novo entrepreneurial ventures that are financed externally and corporate entrepreneurial ventures that are financed internally, the fundamental problem of creating legitimacy remains.

5.2.3 Option 3: Linking the Organization to the Environment

Skunk works and retrofits, like the dominant organizational logic they attempt to circumvent, all rely on a singular selection regime, whether it be the entrepreneur's own belief set, the organization's official strategy, or the entrepreneur's attempt to contort the later into the former. Consider the feedback processes and selection criteria implied by such singularity. One basis of evaluation is an untested belief about the market. Such beliefs may well persist as a result of the failure to test them (Weick, 1979; Denrell and March, 2001), unless proven to the contrary via vicarious learning from others. The other selection criterion corresponds to fitness with respect to the organization's ongoing policies and, more broadly, conception of itself. Clearly, this latter selection criterion is also not likely to introduce novelty nor act as a source of change for an organization.

An alternative to these internally focused regimes is tight coupling to the external product market (Adner and Levinthal, 2002). While organizations may have a focus on a particular conception of their "core competencies" or defining markets and mission, there is one common denominator across all business firms—and that is money. A projection onto the performance dimension of financial return provides a credible statement of value regardless of how far-fetched or seemingly unrelated an initiative may be. Further, the external market in which success and failure are ultimately evaluated is a highly variegated environment. This variegated environment suggests the possibility of making use of the heterogeneity of the demand landscape itself to create support for "other" directed ventures.

The recent attention to the phenomena of lean start-ups (Reiss, 2011) is interesting to consider in this regard. This approach is premised on the role of direct feedback from market trials as to the merits of either the incipient product technology and its features or the market application to which this effort is directed. Not only is there an emphasis on the role of feedback versus ex-ante beliefs as to the merits of one approach or another, the idea that there is a large set of potential niches to which the effort might be applied as well as a wide variety of possible variants of the initiative itself is central to the approach. But another critical assumption in this approach, often not highlighted in these discussions, is that experimenting in situ in the market will provide rapid, and reasonably reliable, feedback as to the merit of a particular offering (Contigiani and Levinthal, 2019). However, many of the economic actions in which we are most interested have the property that their full implications are not realized until some future time period. This is particularly true in the context of the development of new technologies where contemporaneous market feedback regarding possible merit is not feasible or at least may not be reliable.

The direct linkage to product and financial markets is at times achieved by the formation of a new, distinct organizational form largely decoupled from the authority structure of the corporate office. Such ventures may be kept within the existing organization (e.g. Block and Macmillan, 1993) or managed as partial spinoffs (e.g. Chesbrough, 2002). Corporate venture funds that invest in promising internal and external initiatives have become a vehicle to achieve such direct linkage (e.g. Dushnitsky and Lenox, 2005). Dushnitsky and Shapira (2010) observe that corporate venture capital organizations are often required to find private venture partners to invest alongside them, not just to spread risk, but to safeguard against possibly biased value assessments. Such externalization of corporate initiatives provides a partial, but not complete, degree of decoupling from the firm's existing strategic context; but, at the same time, these structures impose some elements of discipline from product market competition and the evaluation of financial markets. However, per the discussion in the prior chapter regarding the timing of selection forces in the context of unfolding development efforts, this direct linking to the environment offers the possibility of a heterogeneity of bases of evaluation but also poses the potential risk of the myopic selection force of current product market feedback.

5.3 Ecology of Dimensions

Framing the contrast between exploration and exploitation as stemming in part from a contestation around what constitutes appropriate and valuable dimensions of performance might suggest expanding the set of performance dimensions. Unfortunately, the solution to this challenge of differing world views cannot simply be that organizations adopt the union of all performance dimensions that are relevant to the set of actors with whom they are interacting.

There are two basic reasons for this restriction of attention. First, boundedly rational actors are restricted to low-dimensional representations of more complex realities (Gärdenfors, 2000). Thus, while it is fashionable to scoff at the simple 2×2 representations that are common in the strategy field, it is important to recognize that individuals are hard pressed to think simultaneously about many more dimensions than that. Halford et al. (1994) find that the most complex statistical relationship that individuals can process in working memory is a three-way interaction (i.e. three independent variables and one dependent variable, for a total of four dimensions). Thus, there is an important opportunity cost in adding additional dimensions: the risk of adopting a dimension of performance that is not well aligned with the space of economic payoffs and the addition of a dimension that effectively crowds out a possibly more valuable basis by which to judge performance.

Furthermore, additional dimensions of performance pose additional hazards to coordinated action within an organization. Strategy, and the set of operational goals, should direct and coordinate action among a disparate group of individuals. As more dimensions are added, attention is inevitably fragmented and the level of coordination reduced. Attempting to focus simultaneously on a broad array of performance measures can effectively freeze an adaptive system (Ethiraj and Levinthal, 2009). Ethiraj and Levinthal (2009) demonstrate in a computational model that providing actors with a highly restricted subset of the true goal structure can facilitate adaptive learning even as judged by the criterion of the full goal structure. Consistent with this argument, Obloj and Sengul (2020) find in their study of French manufacturers that increasing the number of goals decreases performance on any given focal performance dimension.

Organizations facilitate coordinated actions among disparate individuals and subgroups. This coordination is achieved through the alignment of interests and beliefs, with the former challenge typically thought of as resolved, or at least mitigated, through some form of incentive alignment (Gibbons and Roberts, 2013). Socialization processes may also mitigate the challenge of goal conflict through the development of shared identity that in turn may serve to achieve a greater degree of shared motives (Van Mannen, 1973; Ouchi, 1980). Strategy is an important mechanism to align and direct behavior within organizations. As such, a strategy serves to define and legitimate the dimensions along which progress is to be measured. In so doing, of course, a given strategy also acts to de-legitimate alternative dimensions along which progress could have been made.

This argumentation regarding the appropriate bases by which to evaluate performance occurs not only within firms, but also with respect to financial markets' evaluation of firms. Despite their independence from a specific strategic mandate, investors in the financial markets need to rely on metrics of performance as well. The need to establish the legitimacy of such dimensions and to navigate deviations from established benchmarks is present in both internal and external resource markets. For example, Gurley (1999) argues that a key part of McCaw's success in the cable industry and then in cellular was his ability to convince financial markets of the appropriateness of non-financial measures of performance, such as "homes-passed" in the context of cable and "POPs," or percent of population served, in the context of cellular, as opposed to traditional financial measures such as the price-earnings relationship. As capital-intensive businesses, cable and cellular required enormous sums of investment prior to significant evidence of financial return. McCaw was able to convince investors to accept these alternatives as substitutes so that "even though these companies may have been hemorrhaging cash, investors could now take comfort that a cable franchise was worth $2,000 per home passed, or that a wireless company was worth $30 per POP (percentage of population)" (Gurley, 1999).

Entrepreneurship is about novel acts. However, the novelty of the behavior does not in and of itself constitute entrepreneurship. Moving along existing technological trajectories or extending existing business models may impose tremendous individual and organizational demands. There may be questions of the feasibility of these initiatives and uncertainty as to their payoff on the existing agreed-upon performance criteria. However, claims about the value of new dimensions of performance are arguably a more fundamental source of novelty.

Entrepreneurs, whether inside an existing entity or in the process of forming a new entity, often have a distinct vision. They may see the payoff space in a different light than other actors and pursue avenues of progress along those dimensions of perceived value. However, entrepreneurs cannot act in a vacuum. Effective entrepreneurs, whether inside the corporate context or external to it, must acquire sufficient material and financial resources to sustain their efforts. To do so in the immediate term, they must validate their endeavor in terms that a "Flatlander" can appreciate. In the longer term, there is the possibility of transforming perceptions of the payoff surface itself. While we are all condemned to live in "flatlands" as our understanding of performance metrics is inevitably of very modest dimensionality, projecting the true business landscape on different bases can offer radically different representations of the payoff service (Csaszar and Levinthal, 2016). The low-dimensional representation of the space is not discretionary, but arguably the most powerful form of entrepreneurship are cognitive shifts that offer a different topology of the business landscape.

5.4 Summary

This chapter offers a reconceptualization of processes of exploration and exploitation. While traditionally processes of exploration and exploitation have been understood with respect to the novelty of the associated behavior and the a priori beliefs of the promise of that behavior from the perspective of the focal actor, the perspective developed here highlights the possible contestation regarding the merit and promise of a given action or initiative. In particular, it is argued that a given action may be viewed as exploratory from one party's perspective, often observers of the behavior, while that same action may be considered exploitive from the perspective of the focal actor. This perspective on exploration and exploitation is not intended to supplant the existing treatment of this tension; rather, the argument developed here is intended to supplement that perspective. The argument developed here shifts the contestation from the realm of alternative behaviors to the interpretation of the outcomes of those behaviors and, relatedly, highlights the alternative a priori beliefs and cognitive schemas by which promising behaviors and initiatives are evaluated. Validating actions to others, either ex ante or ex post, requires either the validation of particular dimensions of performance or the casting of "shadows" on the dimension of performance valued by others.

Exploration and Exploitation: Arms versus Tress

The fundamental tension between exploration and exploitation has, from early on, been formalized as corresponding to an n-armed bandit problem (Holland, 1975; Gittins, 1979). The bandit formulation captures important elements of this tradeoff: the choice of one-armed is treated as precluding the choice of some latent alternative arm and learning about the possible merits of alternative arms requires their use or experimentation. However, embedded in the n-armed structure are a number of properties, properties that have assumed a kind of taken-for-granted nature, that arguably do not reflect central characteristics of managerial and strategic decision-making.

Perhaps most importantly, the bandit set-up implies the possibility of return. If experimentation with some new sampled option provides unfavorable results, the actor is treated as having the option to return to the prior action. Furthermore, if subsequent draws on this prior action drive down beliefs about its merits, there is the further possibility of revisiting this formerly "rejected" alternative. Path-dependence is present in bandit models with regard to how beliefs are shaped over time and, in turn, how those beliefs influence future choices of actions. The hot-stove effect that Denrell and March (2001) analyze is a particularly strong manifestation of this form of path-dependence. Denrell and March note that a negative realization of a newly sampled option may dissuade an actor from trying this option in the future and possibly correcting what may be a mistaken negative assessment.

However, path-dependence is absent in arguably a more fundamental sense. The latent opportunity structure is treated as unchanging over time.[6] If on Monday a certain choice was taken and outcome realized, the other $n-1$ possibilities lie in wait on Tuesday, and Tuesday's choice has no impact on the possibility of action on Wednesday. This characterization may seem to trivialize the issue by the use of days of the week to mark time periods; however, the fundamental issue clearly remains if one expresses the choice structure over time in more general terms as a "period." Such a dynamic certainly seems apt for a decision such as what constitutes the best path and mode of transit by which to commute to work. The pain, pleasure, and time associated with the different possibilities can be sampled and revisited, with the choice of not engaging in a particular option in a given time period not precluding that possibility in a future time period.

This history-invariant opportunity structure, however, seems at odds with our usual conception of actors needing to "seize" opportunities. The notion that it is important to "seize" an opportunity presumably stems from a sense that an actor may be faced with some unique opportunity structure that may not, and indeed may be unlikely to, present itself again in the future. A latent entrepreneur coming of age at the dawn of the PC (e.g. Gates [Microsoft], Jobs [Apple]), the Internet (e.g. Andreessen [Netscape], Case [AOL]), or ecommerce (e.g. Bezos [Amazon], Omidyar

Continued

---

[6] There are models that incorporate the possibility that the value associated with a given "arm" may change over time (Whittle, 1988; Posen and Levinthal, 2012). However, it is still the case that in these models, the opportunity to engage in any one of the n-possible actions is present each period.

Continued

[eBay]) may face a unique historical circumstance. If one of these actors decided to pass on that latent opportunity in some "period *t*" to experience further their current situation or some third alternative, that latent opportunity would not necessarily be lying in wait for them at some future "period *t+1*." Further, seizing this opportunity will entail negating other latent choices, for some continuing with their education and for others existing employment, or again some alternative "outside option"—that is something distinct from their current choice at time *t* and this particular latent opportunity.

Rather than conceiving exploration and exploitation as a sampling problem, and again a sampling dynamic with no fundamental path-dependence, consider instead the sort of branching process that evolutionary biologists term phylogenetic trees, or sometimes more colloquially the "tree of life" (Dennett, 1995). The hierarchical nature of such "trees" indicates ancestry, while the branching connotes speciation events.[7] While in the biological context this branching is a random process of genetic variety in conjunction with some possible happenstance of the particular niche space in which the new form arrives, in the organizational context such "branching" may reflect considerable intentionality. However, that intentionality may occur in the context of highly uncertain opportunity structure, as noted in the different epochs of opportunity in information technology.

The entrepreneurs noted above moved into the adjacent possible (Kauffman, 2000). Changes in the broader macro environment of technology and the business context made possible these initiatives, initiatives which just a few years prior would have not been feasible. Further, per the notion of a "window of opportunity," if they as latent entrepreneurs had waited, perhaps per the sensibility of the exploration/exploitation trade-off not wanting to give up their current activity, that opportunity would soon pass—either because other actors would move to realize its potential, or if there was a substantial "collective" waiting on the part of the full

---

[7] The concept of speciation events and its relationship to processes of organizational evolution are developed in the following chapter.

set of latent entrepreneurs, changes in technology and the business context might render the opportunity moot.

For our purposes, it may be better to relabel the "tree of life" a "tree of opportunities." More accurately, the "tree" reflects those opportunities that were realized—presumably out of a vast sea of latent opportunities. There is not some constant number of "arms" over which choice occurs, but an everchanging array of latent and realized trajectories. In addition, as is true in the case of phylogenetic trees in evolutionary biology, branches do not extend forever. Clearly, a branch may simply terminate as the result of an extinction event—and what we might think of in the business context less dramatically as an exit, if one thinks of the branch as an initiative within the firm, or the demise of an industry, if one is thinking of organizational populations. Branches may also terminate with what evolutionary biologist would term a speciation event. A speciation event can take on two basic forms. One is akin to what discussions in entrepreneurship and "lean startups" would term a "pivot." There is an abrupt shift in the trajectory, but not a formation of a new distinct branch. Alternatively, as is a common situation in the context of corporate entrepreneurial activity, the initiation of a new line of business is not necessarily tied to the termination of an existing business unit and thus the existing trajectory may persist with a branching event—a new initiative that supplements prior initiatives.

The breadth of a corporate "tree" of activity is presumably a joint function of resource availability and the relative opportunity represented by each of the extant "branches." Within the context of lean startups, it is argued that the enterprise should focus on a single initiative at any point in time. In that setting, the need for focus is driven by the limited resources of the enterprise. If progress is to be made along a trajectory, the suggestion is that there needs be a single trajectory. The link between progress and focus is not merely one of resources, but also the sense of "burning bridges" behind oneself by foregoing prior trajectories presumably acts as an important incentive (Shin and Milkman, 2016).

A more established enterprise, as noted, can sustain some multiplicity of initiatives at any given time; however, the constraints and opportunity costs of scarce talent, time, and "treasure" are still present (Levinthal and

Continued

Continued

Wu, 2010). Because the formal modeling apparatus of the bandit model treats choice as being discrete, one of n options, the issue of the scale of activity is not present in discussions of the exploration/exploitation trade-off. But the issue is not simply whether activity $i, j,$ or k is engaged in, but what is the allocation of capital and managerial time and bandwidth associated with each. Somewhat similarly, in the representation of phylogenetic trees in evolutionary biology, the "branch" represents the presence of a particular form, but there is no recognition in this schema of the scale, or density, of forms.

6

Punctuated Change

The pace of change is a central question regarding evolutionary dynamics. While the perspective put forth by Darwin was one of descent with modification, this view was supplemented by Gould and Eldredge's theory of punctuated equilibrium (Eldredge and Gould, 1972 and Gould and Eldredge, 1977). The idea of punctuated equilibrium has, in turn, had important influence in the management field. Discussions of technological evolution, for instance, often describe the technology life cycle as characterized by periods of incremental innovation that are punctuated by sudden bursts of radical innovations (e.g. Abernathy and Utterback, 1978; Tushman and Anderson, 1986; Anderson and Tushman, 1990; Mokyr, 1990). Similarly, organizational theorists (e.g. Miller and Friesen, 1980; Tushman and Romanelli, 1985; Gersick, 1988, 1991; Romanelli and Tushman, 1994) have proposed a punctuated model of organizational transformation, arguing that organizations evolve through relatively long periods of stability marked by short bursts of fundamental change.

There are three basic arguments underlying punctuated equilibrium theory as developed by Gould and Eldredge: the pace of evolutionary change, the role of speciation events, and the relationship between micro and macro evolutionary processes. However, the management literature has generally focused on only the first of these. In contrast, work in evolutionary biology has highlighted the critical role of all three mechanisms of evolutionary change and in particular the role of speciation (Stebbins and Ayala, 1981). Indeed, Mayr (1988: 483) suggests that "speciational evolution" may be a better term for the process Gould and Eldredge characterize than punctuated equilibrium. As a result, it is important to consider with care the processes and mechanisms that underlie the notion of "punctuated change."

As suggested by the above discussion, we need to be careful as to what does and does not constitute a punctuation event. In early writings within evolutionary biology, the notion was put forward of "hopeful monsters," new forms that result from mutations involving genes that control development entailing broad-scale change in the phenotype (Goldschmidt, 1940). This perspective was then imported into the management literature with regard to both organizational form (Tushman and Romanelli, 1985; Romanelli and Tushman, 1994) and technological change (Mokry, 1991). According to such arguments, while microevolution can occur by natural selection of small genetic variants, more dramatic change occurs by a different process (i.e. via hopeful monsters). Mokyr (1991), in his analysis of technological change, makes this argument explicit and distinguishes between macroinventions (the analog of macromutations) that create a new technology (the analog of a new species) and microinventions (i.e. gradual accumulation of novelties) that refine and improve existing technologies. Without discarding the possibility that a new technology can also emerge by the accumulation of small inventions, he maintains that the term "hopeful monstrosity" seems an apt description of such revolutionary inventions as "Gutenberg's first printing press or Newcomen's 1712 Dudley Castle machine" (1991: 142).

As a rare theoretical possibility, macromutations in evolutionary biology cannot be ruled out. However, the likelihood of a macromutation generating novel adaptations would appear to be exceedingly small. This point is nicely captured by Dawkins's distinction between Boeing 747 macromutations and Stretched DC8 macromutations. Boeing 747 macromutations are ruled out by the complexity inherent in their happenstance: the idea of "a single macromutation's giving rise to a fully functioning eye... is, indeed, just about as improbable as a hurricane assembling a Boeing 747. This is why I refer to this kind of hypothetical macromutations as a Boeing 747 macromutation" (Dawkins, 1987: 234). Stretched DC8 macromutations, on the contrary, are large with respect to the magnitude of their effects, but not as complex as the former. A Stretched DC8 is basically an airliner that "was made by modifying an earlier airliner, the DC8. It is like a DC8, but with an elongated fuselage" (Dawkins, 1987: 234–5). Dawkins (1987: 236) goes further to argue that Stretched DC8 macromutations are macromutations only "if we look, naively, at the finished product, the adult. If we look at the processes of embryonic development they turn out to be micromutations, in the sense that only a small change in the embryonic instructions had a large apparent effect in the adult." In this spirit, the belief that certain innovations are generated by revolutionary upheavals in technology can arguably be traced to a concealment of crucial antecedents (Basalla, 1988).

If macromutations are not the primary cause of speciation, or they are only under extraordinary circumstances, other mechanisms or evolutionary forces must be able to explain the dynamics of the process. The notion of ecological speciation is introduced here to shed light on some of the crucial mechanisms underlying these dynamics. An important implication of this argument is that seemingly "discrete" or discontinuous evolutionary changes can occur without invoking any role for macromutations. This argument is developed to consider change processes in three different contexts: the pace of technological change, shifts in organizational strategy and capabilities, and changes in the scope of firms.[1]

6.1 Punctuated Equilibrium Processes in Management

6.1.1 Technological Change

Discussions of technological change have offered sharply contrasting perspectives. On the one hand, we have arguments regarding the gradual, incremental nature of technological change

---

[1] This discussion draws from Levinthal (1998), Adner and Levinthal (2002), and Cattani and Levinthal (2005).

(Dosi, 1983; Basalla, 1988). In contrast, others have offered the image of technological change as being rapid, even discontinuous (Tushman and Anderson, 1986; D'Aveni, 1994). Indeed, the locus classicus of evolutionary perspectives of technological change (Schumpeter, 1934) offers the dramatic imagery of "waves of creative destruction."

Levinthal (1998) builds on Gould and Eldridge's (1977) argument regarding speciation in reconciling these seemingly divergent perspectives. Discontinuities are generally not the product of singular events in the development of a technology. As in the process of punctuation in the biological context, the critical factor is often a speciation event, the application of existing technological know-how to a new domain of application. Unlike in the biological context, this "speciation" event may be far from random. Indeed, speciation is another way to think of Schumpeter's discussion of the critical element of entrepreneurship consisting of "creative recombinations" of technologies and markets. The entrepreneurial context differs from the biological in that there is conscious intent by actors considering the "adjacent possible" (Kauffman, 2000). The critical element of Schumpeter's argument is that the innovation is a recombination event—a recombining of existing elements. Further, per the notion of speciation, taking an existing technology with some modest modification to a new application domain is a particular kind of recombination.

Speciation events may be the outcome of intentional acts; however, note that "intelligent" speciation only requires a form of local rationality. It need not imply, for instance, that actors made investment in antecedent capabilities with the intent that such capabilities could be used in a novel domain, but merely that they exploit prior cumulated adaptations to the current opportunities. Within evolutionary biology, such a process is termed exaptation, a process whereby a feature selected for in one context or application is found to have value in another, such as fins that evolved for navigating through water for fish becoming wings for land-borne animals (i.e. birds). Cattani (2005) provides a detailed examination of such dynamics in the context of Corning, a materials science-based firm with cookware as one of its key products, becoming a pioneer in fiber optics.[2]

The heavy "lift" of technological development is generally supported by the antecedent market applications; however, these developments may create the "fodder" for these subsequent recombinations. For instance, global positioning systems were not created to facilitate cell phone calls or as a means of targeted marketing to potential customers, but the enormous investments motivated by space exploration and defense systems created a technological platform from which relatively incremental investments and creative insight regarding possible application domains opened up a wide variety of new markets.[3]

While the technological change associated with the shift in domain is typically relatively minor, and in that regard the initial speciation event is quite conservative, it may have significant commercial impact, which in turn may trigger a substantially new and divergent evolutionary trajectory. An initial speciation event is minor in the sense that the technological form does not differ substantially from its predecessor. However, the lineage development of a technology within a new domain of application may differ quite radically from this antecedent technology. First, the new domain of application may have a distinct basis of selection. For instance, the critical attributes of functionality and degree of price sensitivity are likely to differ substantially across domains. Second, domains may differ substantially in the resources associated with them. A modest niche may only sustain a moderate rate of technological progress; while, in contrast, a more mainstream market may permit a much faster pace of development. Thus, while

---

[2] This contrast between ex-post exploitation of unforeseen opportunities and the ex-ante investment in capabilities to potentially exploit some anticipated possible future state distinguishes investments that can be viewed as real options, which assumes a clear intentionality about possible downstream applications when the initial investments are made (Adner and Levinthal, 2004), and acts of exaptation.

[3] It is important to note in this context that while enormous capital expense was made in the "roll out" of this technological platform, these investments were made subsequent to the niche of cell phone use being made feasible by the technological investments outside this domain and, as illustrated in Figure 6.1 below, was part of the "lineage" development of cell phones.

the successful invasion of an existing niche is the dramatic event on which commentators tend to focus, this dramatic event is the outcome of a substantial period of development in a relatively isolated niche. Figure 6.1 illustrates the basic structure of this argument.

The process of "creative destruction" occurs when the technology that emerges from the speciation event is successfully able to invade other niches, possibly including the original domain of application. This is the situation that Christensen and Rosenbloom (1995) identified in the disk drive industry, where the drives developed for the initial niche market of portable computers ultimately became viable in the mainstream desktop market. However, such "invasion" of the original, or predecessor, application domain need not occur (Adner, 2002; Adner and Zemsky, 2005) as the domains may differ sufficiently in their selection criteria that the two forms can coexist.

This history of wireless communication technology provides a useful context with which to illustrate this argument. The large technological shifts that transpired over time in the development of this technology are generally regarded as "revolutionary"; however, a closer examination reveals a more nuanced and gradual

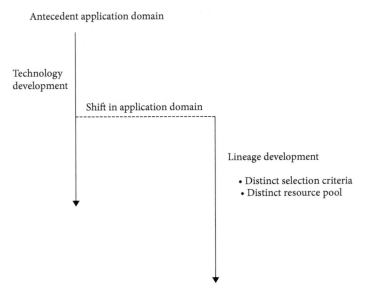

Figure 6.1 Speciation in technological development.

evolutionary dynamic, with speciation playing a critical role (Levinthal, 1998). We see from Marconi adopting Hertz's laboratory equipment to provide the initial wireless telegraphy, to the subsequent advances in wireless telegraphy, and in particular the innovation of a continuous wave transmitter being applied by a Westinghouse engineer to radio broadcasting, existing technologies were reapplied to new application domains with dramatic commercial and technological consequences. Further, these novel repurposing events were associated with modest incremental technical efforts at the point of entry into the new application domain.

These "revolutions" in communication technology were, in a technical sense, incremental: an existing technology was ported to a new application domain. However, once shifted to a new domain, a distinct and, in many cases, rapid path of lineage development ensued, driven both by the distinct selection or performance criteria of the new domain, as well as the potential financial resources available in the distinct application domains. While Hertz had to make do with make-shift lab equipment, Marconi had the backing of the British Admiralty and later a public company. Radio broadcasting was initiated by a Westinghouse engineer as a hobby, but was then quickly adopted by Sarnoff at RCA, RCA having been previously founded to pursue wireless telegraphy.

6.1.2   Organizational Transformation

The punctuated equilibrium model has been proposed not only in the sphere of technological change, but for organizational change as well (e.g. Miller and Friesen, 1980; Tushman and Romanelli, 1985; Gersick, 1991; Romanelli and Tushman, 1994). Organizations are described as evolving through relatively long periods of stability that are punctuated by relatively short bursts of fundamental change. As Miller and Friesen (1980) argue, organizational change is characterized "by periods of dramatic revolution in which there are reversals in the direction of change across a significantly large number of variables of strategy and structure" (1980: 593). Dwindling performance, major changes in the environment, or firm leadership (e.g. CEO's succession) have all been characterized as potential "triggers" to overcome organizational inertia and stimulate fundamental transformations. As a result, the departure from previous directions of evolution involves "the creation of a new gestalt among variables of strategy, structure, and environment" (Miller and Friesen, 1980: 607).

Despite its wide acceptance, descriptions of punctuated equilibrium in organizational theory generally fall short of fully clarifying the processes and basic mechanisms central to any evolutionary theory. Lichtenstein (1995: 292) puts forward a strong critique:

> In punctuated equilibrium no variations emerge, and no selection mechanisms are defined. At the group level one new framework emerges (from where?) and is instantly chosen. At the organizational level, evolution occurs through a wholesale importing of new activities (or leadership) into the organization, not through a selection process on variations within the activity domains. It's not evident how this is a comparable instance of "evolution" in the neo-Darwinian sense.

The appeal of the punctuated equilibrium model to explain such transformations is evocative in that it reminds us that organizations at times do indeed undergo periods of substantial change; however, the sort of change proposed in these arguments is of a "hopeful monster" variety. While constituting deliberate attempts at adjusting to (and possibly re-establishing a fit with) an evolving environment, one should not presume that such efforts will be adaptive in the sense of ex-post leading to an enhanced fit with the environment and increased likelihood of survival. The application of the concept of punctuated equilibrium requires more than one level of analysis. As a result, as Lichtenstein (1995) notes, arguments that operate solely at the group or organization level inevitably fail to connect with the notion of speciation as a critical driver of evolutionary change.

One possible approach to apply the framework of punctuated change to organizational change is to consider the selection environment within the organization itself. A shift in selection criteria at the organizational level, perhaps corresponding to a change in top management or strategy as suggested by Tushman and Romanelli (1985), could lead to the emergence of a distinct "form." However, note that such a process is conservative regarding processes of change and in particular does not presume or require a "macromutation." Rather, as a result of a change in selection criteria, the firm's resource allocation process (Bower, 1970) would shift the availability of resources across the firm's initiatives and, over time, might result in a distinct and, at least from the firm's point of view, novel set of activities.

Burgelman's (1994) account of Intel's shift from the dwindling DRAM market to the microprocessor market is illustrative in this regard. Intel managers followed a simple production rule, maximizing "margin-per-wafer-start," to determine the resource allocation for manufacturing capacity. By following this simple prioritization, Intel began re-allocating resources and producing proportionally more microprocessors when in the early 1980s margins for memory chips decreased and margins for microprocessors increased. In this case, the selection criteria, "margin-per-wafer-start," remained constant; but it allowed the shift in economic forces to be reflected internally within the firm and led to a radical re-orientation of the firm's production and marketing resources.

Organizational-level politics and the shifting of dominant coalitions can serve as a catalyst to punctuation events as driven by a shift in selection criteria. Political processes are interesting in this regard. If one conceives of politics as reflecting a central tendency of some possibly shifting distribution of preferences, then the associated shift in selection criteria would often be gradual. However, if one conceives of politics as the formation of a dominant coalition (March, 1962), then a reconfiguration of that coalition could lead to discrete shift in priorities and objectives and in turn the selection criteria by which resources are allocated and outcomes are judged. In terms of managerial systems, we might contrast a consensus-based system as reflecting the former sort of process and a hierarchical authority structure as having qualities of the later. In a hierarchical structure, what perspective forms a majority in the boardroom, who is the CEO, and the possible shift in such a majority or role occupant could foreshadow a distinctly new evolutionary trajectory for the organization.

6.1.3 Speciation and Firm Diversification

The notion of speciation has important implications for research on diversification, particularly from the perspective of the resource-based view of the firm (e.g. Penrose, 1959; Barney, 1991). The logic of diversification in this line of research stems from some form of resource leverage across product markets. Further, these distinct market contexts are likely to pose divergent selection environments.

Recognizing diversification as being driven by a process of speciation helps reconcile two robust, but seemingly conflicting empirical findings. One finding is that firms tend to diversify into related domains (e.g. Teece et al., 1994; Puranam and Vanneste, 2016). Yet, at the same time, empirical evidence suggests that very little of the diversity of business units' performance can be attributed to their corporate identity (Rumelt, 1991; McGahan and Porter, 1997; Vanneste, 2017). However, both sets of findings are exactly what one would expect if diversification is driven by speciation events. Firms face the opportunity to apply their resources and capabilities to related domains or niches. However, given that these new efforts are subject to a distinct set of selection forces, a qualitatively distinct form (where in the context of firm diversification, a "form" can be thought of as a distinct business unit) is likely to emerge. On an ongoing basis, the further lineage development and ongoing operations of the originating business unit may have minimal interrelationship with the subsequent lineage development of the new business unit. Thus, relatedness should predict the likelihood of speciation events; but, since speciation necessitates the presence of divergent selection pressures, there is no reason to anticipate significant performance linkages across the distinct forms (business units) in subsequent time periods.

Consider, for instance, General Electric, historically one of the most widely diversified U.S. business firms. Many of the businesses that GE entered, such as power generation equipment, medical imaging, appliances, GE Capital, seem to have little or no operational relationship to one another. However, the initiation of the bulk of GE's business units can be seen as speciation events stemming from a prior lineage of capability development. GE was founded to develop and commercialize the innovations of Thomas Edison, most importantly electric lighting and electricity generation. Edison's and subsequently GE's interest in the dynamo as a source of power for electrical devices led to the firm's work in small electric motors and in turn the development of the small appliance business, starting with electric fans in the 1890s.[4] More surprising are the early roots of GE's efforts in plastics, which stemmed from Edison's experiments with plastic filaments for light bulbs in 1893, and ultimately led to the first GE Plastics department created in 1930. Similarly, the invention of the X-ray tube in the early 1910s originated from previous work done at GE in the field of tungsten-filament for incandescent electric lighting (Reich, 1985).

While there is a resource leverage logic that can explain GE's entry into these diverse businesses, once these business units fully take shape in the pursuit of their distinct market niches, there is little ongoing connection to the antecedent businesses that facilitated the original diversification. Thus, the new businesses come to comprise a distinct "form" within the context of GE—the outcome of the divergent selection forces of the distinct product markets that these business units aim to serve. In other words, a speciation event occurred.

6.2 Summary

Upheavals in organizations and technologies have often been viewed as equivalent to macromutations. Changes in organizational power structures and strategy, just as changes in the application domains for technologies, are often discrete events that can have profound implications for subsequent evolutionary dynamics. However, it is important to note that such events are typically "genetically" conservative. An organization may change its power structure and its strategy overnight, but its capability set the "next morning" is likely to look very much like its capability set the prior day. By recognizing the multi-level nature of these processes, we

---

[4] Source: http://www.ge.com/en/company/companyinfo/at_a_glance/history_story.htm.

can reconcile our often conflicting sense of organizations and technologies as undergoing periods of rapid change, while still conforming to a gradualist perspective with regard to the underlying "genetic" level of underlying firm capabilities and technological trajectories. Rather than arguing about the gradual or discontinuous nature of organizational transformations and technological change, an arguably more fruitful approach is to delve more deeply into the underlying mechanisms producing them. Speciation is a critical link between these micro-level processes and macroevolutionary change. Punctuated equilibrium is a powerful and insightful concept; however, its effective application ultimately requires its reconnection with ideas of Darwinian gradualism. This has proved true in evolutionary biology and should prove true in the management literature as well.

Punctuated Change and Nested Systems of Adaptation

In considering the pace of change, it is important recognize organizations as constituting multi-level systems that themselves are embedded in some environmental context. The schema in Figure 6.2 provides a minimal structure, specifying three different levels of analysis: underlying elements, organizational selection criteria, and the selection pressures of the niche in which the organization operates. Many discussions within the management literature that adopt the term "punctuated" change reference change in the underlying elements (Tushman and Romanelli, 1985; Gersick, 1988;

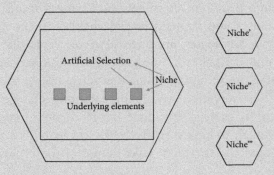

Figure 6.2   Nested systems of selection.

Romanelli and Tushman, 1994). While such "macromutations" are possible (Goldschmidt, 1940) their appearance, at least in a functional performance-enhancing manner, is rather unlikely (Dawkins, 1987). Rather, the discrete change associated with punctuation is associated with a shift in the selection criteria guiding the evolution of these underling elements.

There are two distinct fulcrums by which these criteria might shift. One lies within the organization itself. This is what we have referred to as the artificial selection environment of the organization. What projects and initiatives within the organization are deemed more or less valuable? What kinds of group and individual outcomes should be strongly reinforced through compensation and promotion practices? One could imagine these selection criteria shifting in some gradual manner, placing incrementally more or less weight on one sort of performance criteria or another. However, one can also imagine that these shifts could be more substantial and dramatic. This is easy to see in the context of political systems operating under a majority rule structure, where the exit of one political party and the entrance of another can generate quite discrete changes in resources and the evaluation of initiatives. What policies are promulgated and adopted can change quite dramatically even if the underlying bureaucracy and organizational machinery remain fairly stable. Shifts in top management teams, and associated shifts in vision and strategy, can have similar consequences for business enterprises.

Hierarchies are multi-level systems. Typically, we envision ideas and proposals drifting upwards (Bower, 1970; Rivkin and Siggelkow, 2003; Ganz, 2018) and these ideas screened by actors higher in the system (Knudsen and Levinthal, 2007; Christensen and Knudsen, 2010). A change in selection criteria by actors at the higher rungs of such a hierarchy change the resulting demography of initiatives through the differentiated screening criteria applied to proposals and initiatives to which they are presented. In addition, there may be some endogeneity in what constitutes this population of proposals and initiatives, with actors generating possibilities that they perceive as consonant with a given set of screening criteria. Actors are likely to anticipate the criteria by which their initiatives are judged and mold them accordingly.

Continued

Continued

The role of the niche is twofold. On the one hand, the selection pressures of the niche within which the organization is operating may exert force on the organization's artificial selection environment. It is certainly the case that an organization's artificial selection environment can be somewhat decoupled from the external environment. Indeed, such decoupling is central to the notion of the organization making strategic choices (Hrebeniak and Joyce, 1985). In the absence of any decoupling, the organization's choice processes would be wholly determined by the properties of the environment in which the organization is operating. Such decoupling might be associated with visionary strategic leadership, positioning the organization for what the selection pressure in the niche might look like in the future—a future perhaps entailing important technological or regulatory changes. However, such decoupling can also apply pressure on current organizational performance. To be not well aligned with current customer preferences, stock investors' perspectives, and the like can entail considerable financial pain (Benner and Ranganathan, 2013). This "pain" might prompt the organization to modify its artificial selection environment. It is this pressure of the niche on the organization that is represented by the arrow in Figure 6.2 going from niche to artificial selection.

The niche can also operate directly on the initiatives themselves, the "underlying elements." This possibility was raised in the prior chapter in the context of how budding corporate intrapreneurs might validate their initiatives that lie outside the organization's strategic priorities. Business units receive more or less revenue as a function of how the market responds to their offerings and the value placed on these offerings by latent customers relative to competitors' offerings. This response is a function of the attributes of these offering and activities and those available in the niche, but is not directly dependent of the organization's strategy—aside from how the strategy might impact the nature of the offering and the activities themselves. Thus, product lines and business units may rise and fall in their commercial performance in ways that are not guided by the firm's strategy or artificial selection environment.

In addition to the organization possibly modifying its internal selection environment, the organization can shift the niche in which it operates, as suggested by the three alternative niches in Figure 6.2. A shift in niche is often what constitutes a "pivot" in the context of lean startups (Ries, 2011). In the context of the development of technologies, such shifts are often thought of as shifts in application domains (Rosenberg, 1963). A new niche, by the arguments noted immediately above, will then exert a different set of direct selection pressures and reinforcement on the specific initiatives and activities within the organization. In addition, a new niche may impact the degree to which the organization's artificial selection process is coupled to the external environment, and if loosely coupled, in what manner. Further, this loose coupling might impact possible changes in the organization's artificial selection.

A central property of a shift in selection criteria, whether the artificial selection environment of the organization or that of the niche in which the organization operates, is that such shifts can be discrete. At one point the organization may value a certain customer segment, or favor a certain technology and technology trajectory; and, at another point, possibly quite close in time, favor a different segment or technological trajectory. Imagine the stylized conception of the organization as an "urn" containing a variety of colored "balls" where the balls are indicative of the demography of projects and initiatives within the organization. A selection scheme that, for instance, favors orange balls over other colors will, over time, generate an organization with a composition of balls of that color. If the organization were to shift at one moment in time to a "green ball" strategy, the demography of balls in the urn at that moment would remain the same. In that sense the shift in strategy, or internal selection criteria, is conservative with respect to the underlying elements of the organization. However, over some time period, with the magnitude of the time period depending on the intensity of this internal selection process, the proportion of orange balls would decline and the organization would start to look like a green ball organization. In that respect, the shift in selection criteria triggers a punctuation event. Through some combination of initiative level change, whether through existing initiatives

Continued

Continued

---

transforming themselves to appear to adhere to the new selection criteria, or existing initiatives compatible with the new selection criteria scaling, or demographic change (i.e. the exit or disbandment of some initiatives and the birthing of others), the overall distribution of activities will shift.

However, the time scale at which these changes occur is generally slower than that by which the selection criteria itself can shift. That is not to say that a shift in selection criteria may not have been preceded by considerable debate and politicking (Kaplan, 2008). However, a shift in what is valued by the organization is not directly constrained by the plasticity of the organization's operating capabilities, which tend to be fairly slow to adapt. To analogize at the level of individual skills, one can decide to learn a foreign language or participate in a new sport and that decision over time will shift how one allocates time and energy and, over time, will lead to a change in the individual's skill set. However, that shift in priorities is on a fundamentally different time scale than the shift in this skill set. While an organization comprising many individuals and having the capacity to acquire people and operating units might be able to change its skill set at a more rapid rate than that of an individual, the time scale at which the capability set evolves is generally considerably different than that of the shift of the selection criteria, whether the internal selection environment or niche. Further, it is the shift in selection criteria that is the catalyst to this shift in capabilities and activities.

7

Modern Mendels and Organizational Adaptation

At the outset of this work, we characterized two divergent poles of bases for intelligence: one a forward-looking, anticipatory mode and the other some mechanism of sifting through experience and prior outcomes. In recent years, there has been a growing interest in the latter form of intelligence, particularly in the context of strategic management. This may stem from a sense that in a business environment that strikes most observers as ever more changing and complex the limits of foresight are even more keenly felt. The management literature is filled with the encouragement to "fail fast" and to treat start-up ventures as experiments that strive to pivot themselves to a satisfactory product-market match (Reiss, 2011). There are also variants of techniques of experiential learning that place greater emphasis on more classic notions of rationality. The use of, and advocacy for, real options is a salient example of such approaches. "Design thinking" (Osborn, 1953; Brown, 2009) represents an interesting hybrid, as a central part of this approach entails a deep engagement in the context of (potential) users' experience; while, at the same time, this data is fodder for "offline," or "whiteboard" ideation exercises. We consider a range of experimental efforts from highly structured experiments of random controlled trials to less structured efforts of pivoting, as well as processes of reinforcement learning, imitation, and recombination and in doing so highlight the role of context-dependence. Building on these arguments, we conclude with some modest propositions for our Mendelian executive.

7.1 Context-Dependence and Processes of Learning

A key challenge in processes of learning is the degree to which one can generalize from a particular instance, the payoff associated with a particular action taken in a specific context, to other settings, where these "other settings" might be different organizations or the same entity at a different point in time. Different mechanisms of learning vary in how they speak to this challenge. In this light, we contrast efforts at random controlled trials to discover general truths versus more narrow cast efforts, such as A/B testing that engage in experiments that speak to the particular context in which they are carried out. These efforts at self-conscious experimentation are then contrasted with non-experimental approaches of reinforcement learning, imitation, and recombination.

7.1.1 Context-dependence and Random Controlled Trails

To address this question, it is useful to start with what constitutes an RCT and some of the taken-for-granted assumptions that often accompany its use.[1] RCTs have risen in popularity in recent years as a way to combat concerns regarding uncontrolled and unmeasured elements of endogeneity in naturally occurring data. Strategies are not randomly allocated to firms. Therefore, when we observe the effectiveness of a particular strategy, it can be challenging to disentangle the merits of the observed strategy versus possibly unmeasured attributes of the organization choosing a particular strategy (Shaver, 1998). The RCT frees one from such concerns by allocating the behavior of interest, a strategy in this context, at random to particular actors. Observations of such samples are argued to provide a clear indication, indeed a causal indication, of the merits of the alternatives considered.

---

[1] This section draws from discussions with Phanish Puranam.

In this regard, RCTs are a powerful engine for insight and understanding. But it is important to note some of the limitations associated with this particular "engine." First, the RCT provides an average effect for a sampled population. This "average" blends the outcomes for experimental subjects for whom the intervention may have yielded a positive or negative effect. This dispersion may solely reflect a stochastic random effect, but it is also possible that the divergence across subjects could be systematic. Indeed, consider some of the challenges in the use of RCTs in what is arguably their source context of the testing of medical interventions. The recent interest in so-called "personalized medication" is an acknowledgment of important elements of heterogeneity within subject pools. A particular medical protocol that has had little efficacy on average may have important therapeutic consequence for specific subpopulations, and there is a risk that latently promising approaches could be cast aside due to the absence of an "average effect." Of course, if one knew the characteristics that defined these distinct subpopulations, the experimental trials could be appropriately stratified, and recent methodological advances are facilitating the partitioning of sample populations based on unobserved treatment effects (Athey and Imbens, 2016).

A related issue is the representativeness of the sample to broader populations to which findings are assumed to apply. If, for instance, one samples college undergraduates in a required psychology class, how indicative are the findings for broader and more diverse populations? Issues of the non-representativeness of samples are gaining attention, whether concerns of race and gender or the U.S.-centric nature of a vast set of strategy research. Researchers are very conscious of sample selection effects in the form of the possible endogeneity of what they might be tempted to treat as an exogenous variable, such as organizational structure or strategy within a given study. However, we as a community of scholars have been relatively acquiescent about the convenience, or saliency-based, choice of samples that are studied.

Both the issue of the limitations of average effects and the potential non-representativeness of the underlying sample of the RCT ultimately relate to a concern with "context dependence." Context

refers here not just to the external setting in which an actor operates but to the particular characteristics of the "subjects." The issue
of this latter form of possible context dependence is particularly
salient in the strategy field, a domain that has privileged the role of
unique, firm-specific factors (Barney, 1991) in accounting for performance difference—the ultimate outcome measure that is generally of interest—as well as strategies and practices that are
co-occurring in complex ways (Porter, 1996).

For these reasons, work that feature RCTs in the management
domain have tended to feature interventions that correspond to
fairly basic operating practices (Bloom et al., 2013). In contrast, if
one reflects on the term "strategic," it is generally applied to settings in which choices have important degrees of spatial and, or
intertemporal linkages (Levinthal, 2000; Leiblein et al., 2018).
Thus, contexts, both current and future, are critical to the payoffs
associated with "strategic" actions. Certainly, to the degree that
RCTs can serve as a useful mechanism with which to identify
possibly universal best-practices these efforts serve a valuable
role. Using best practices is surely superior to the use of less than
best practices. However, given the issue of context dependence,
the applicability of a best practice is restricted to settings in
which the performance effects of that practice are largely independent of the $n-1$ other behaviors with which the organization,
or other organizations, may be engaged (Levinthal, 2000;
Rivkin, 2000).[2]

From the vantage point of an evolutionary approach, a best
practice treats the efficacy of the "gene" or practice as the object of

---

[2] In this regard, it is interesting to consider Mendel's own experimental design. Given his
focus on individual traits, Mendel chose to track seven different attributes in the peas, attributes
that would be readily identifiable. Reflecting this careful choice of traits, Mendel's lab notes
indicate that he initially tracked fifteen traits and then narrowed this down to these seven
(Henig, 2001). A reasonable speculation is that he discarded those traits, including flower
color and pollen shape, that tended to be linked and to be co-occurring and therefore com-
plicated his experimental design. Modern biological research indeed reveals that of the
seven chromosomes constituting a Pisum plant (peas), five of the seven traits on which
Mendel focused are determined by different chromosomes and two are at distant ends of the
same chromosome. Thus, Mendel carefully choose his experimental context to eliminate
interdependencies in the traits that he measured and thereby was able to create an experimental
design whereby inferences regarding the treatment (cross-breeding) versus the controls (his
pure strands) would be clear.

selection. However, in nature, or a naturalistic setting of organizations outside the confines of an RCT, the observed performance is a function of the "phenotype," the entity as whole; or, perhaps at a finer level of aggregation a module, or perhaps individual operating unit or work group within a broader enterprise. Context dependence, in terms of interdependencies with respect to a range of features of the entity for which performance is being evaluated, not only is suggestive of the appropriate unit of aggregation by which outcomes should be evaluated, but similarly is also indicative of the possible merits of processes of replication or imitation. The findings of an RCT, if treated in a context-independent manner, suggests the results as having a universal property. However, if we take context dependence as being important, that implies that the "lessons learned" may be best thought of as being "narrow-cast" to other entities that share a wide set of traits and behavior with the proposed model template of a high-achieving form.

In this regard, it is interesting to contrast RCTs that attempt to identify some general truth to more limited in situ experiments such as A/B testing (Kohavi and Longbothnam, 2017). The A/B testing examines the efficacy of two alternatives in a particular context. For instance, how will sales respond if price is changed in a certain manner, if the web site presents information in a different format, and so on? It is not generally used as a mechanism to identify general findings that might span across settings. In this sense, an A/B test is a form of reinforcement learning but with a degree of parallelism. Two actions are taken and two outcomes are observed and these joint results inform action in that specific context. As a consequence, A/B testing tends to share other attributes of reinforcement learning: the findings reflect context-dependence and the findings provide some suggestion to action but not to causality. Thus, a series of A/B tests might help an organization fine-tune its activity system, but it need not offer some more general insight that would port to other organizations or even potentially to other units of the same organization. In that sense, a pattern of A/B testing offers a means of informed local hill-climbing (Levinthal, 1997).

7.1.2 Reinforcement Learning

Standard processes of reinforcement learning are very much context dependent, both with regard to the set of behaviors and characteristics of the focal entity and the external setting in which the action occurs. An action is taken, possibly a novel action, and if the outcome is viewed as favorable the likelihood of taking that action in the future is increased. The experiment is local and very "site" specific. If action a by actor i is viewed as positive, then actor i is more likely to take action a in the future, or at least in the near-term future. All the ways in which focal actors are embedded in context are incorporated in some fashion in this feedback, whether at the individual level of who else in the organization they are working with in some process of joint production, or the more aggregate level of operating units, the activities of other operating units, or the properties of the niche in which the actors and the organization reside.

While the payoff to that particular action at that moment in time reflects the particular circumstances in which the action takes place, the possible merits of that behavior in future periods hinges to an important degree on whether the critical elements of the context persist from one period to the next. If colleagues with whom one's efforts are interdependent change their behavior, then this effective action in period t may prove less effective in a subsequent time period. This sort of consideration underlines the power of routinized patterns of behavior (Nelson and Winter, 1982). At a more macro level, this potential pathology underlies challenges organizations face when their external context changes, for instance due to "disruptive" technological change (Henderson and Clark, 1990). The issue of appropriate units of aggregation and temporality are not only germane to the various contingencies that might impact performance but, per our earlier discussion of the myopia of learning (Levinthal and March, 1993), to the measures of outcome which form the basis of feedback.

Thus, processes of reinforcement learning are powerful in that they fully incorporate the effect of context in the reinforcement process, but that power is limited to the extent that the current context is less indicative of future contexts. This is true not just for simple processes of reinforcement learning, but for sophisticated processes of machine learning as well, as discussed in the appendix to Chapter 4. The power and effectiveness of machine learning hinges on the degree to which the "training" sample, prior experience, is similar to the "prediction" sample, or future action (Schaffer, 1993). Thus, machine learning is effective in relatively stable environments or contexts.[3] However, as suggested by the power of analogical reasoning (Holyoak and Thagard, 1995; Gavetti et al., 2005) and work on generalization (Sutton, 1996), projecting experience into somewhat distinct novel settings is challenging but possible.

7.1.3 Imitation and Recombination

Much of our experiential wisdom is not self-generated, nor the result of RCTs; rather, a primary engine of progress is imitation— which in the context of an evolutionary process would correspond to differential rates of replication (Hodgson and Knudsen, 2010). In social as opposed to biological systems, this differential replication is generally manifest as processes of imitation. Simple practices such as "copy successful others like you" may be a useful basis of wisdom about appropriate practices. Notice that this is not the same as the injunction to "copy best practice." The modifier "others like you" is a critical part of the claim as it serves as a carrier of the context dependence. Thus, naturally occurring replication is most useful among a population of relative similars. This claim seems quite at odds with our usual understanding regarding the dual power of diversity (Page, 2007) and recombinations (Schumpeter, 1934). For instance, in the context of technological innovation, there is a considerable body of work that suggests that novel linkages of existing ideas and technologies tends to lead to the most promising innovations (Hargadon and Sutton, 1997; Fleming, 2001).

---

[3] This stability of context should be distinguished from the possible dynamics within a context. For instance, a self-driving car must adjust to a very dynamic context of other vehicles, pedestrians, and occasionally malfunctioning traffic signals. However, the algorithms trained to solve the problem of autonomous vehicles are not playing chess tournaments or identifying new pharmaceutical products, so while their focal context has dynamic elements it is a fairly well-circumscribed domain.

To reconcile our conventional wisdom with this provocative suggestion that recombination, and in the limit, replication, among relative similars can be of value, it may be useful to start with a biological example. Evolutionary biologists have long noted the evolutionary power of sexual reproduction versus the biologically possible, and in many species actual, process of asexual reproduction (Barton and Charlesworth, 1998). Sexual reproduction, in contrast to asexual reproduction, adds to the genetic diversity in the subsequent generation through the power of "recombination." However, what has arguably been less appreciated is that this sexual reproduction is not a random matching process, but rather occurs within a single species and indeed is the defining property of what constitutes a species. This is recombination with a strong dose of homophily. Evolutionary biology has developed strong boundary management in that only mating within species is productive.[4]

One might in fact conjecture an optimal degree of similarity within a pool of mutual copiers: they should be similar enough to allow useful copying of a practice that correlates with success—because there is less likely to be idiosyncratic unobserved heterogeneity—but dissimilar enough to produce divergent attempts in the first place—so that novel behaviors can be produced. Homophily-based copying should be robust when there are no significant unobservables that affect action and outcome for the imitatee but not imitator.

More generally, this line of argument suggests a variant, or an analogy, of the classic exploration/exploitation tradeoff. In the argument developed here, mixing and replication among relatively similar others offers a reliability of the merits of actions in a source context for the settings to which those actions might be applied. This greater reliability must be weighed against the value of some degree of variation between the source and "recipient". If the source and recipient setting are identical, we can have the replication of superior practices but the processes of imitation and replication will not generate novelty (Posen et al., 2013). At the same time, if the two settings differ with respect to a number of attributes, then the importing of a policy or set of behaviors from one setting where

---

[4] While there is that interesting familiar anomaly of a mule—the offspring of a male donkey and a female horse—per the spirit our argument, mules themselves cannot reproduce.

the behavior was associated with high performance to another setting need not be functional.

Organizations are interesting "boundary" objects in this regard. Organizations have been recognized as having distinct and persistence cultures and practices. Culture is an important and pervasive context variable: shared values, norms, nuanced form of communication, and the like. Consider what this shared context might imply for the culling of a population of experiments, whether artificially designed randomly controlled trials or naturally occurring less random experiments. Variants that are effective for a single member or subgroup of a broader population of others with whom there is a high degree of shared context, are likely also to be useful variants to draw from for other members and subgroups who share this same context. Furthermore, consider the process of naturally occurring variants and their possible diffusion. As prior research has found, we are generally linked to similar others within an overarching shared context such as an organization (Kleinbaum et al., 2013). To the extent that this is true, the saliency of a successful innovative variant is likely to be correlated with the degree of shared context and therefore this saliency-weighting is likely to be highly aligned with the likelihood of the variant being successful in the potential target population as it was in the initial source. Homophilous copying in this sense acts like a form of representative sampling.

Even within a given organization, there are clearly distinct subcultures (Jermier et al., 1991; Boisnier and Chatman, 2003). These subcultures tend to be linked to the distinct task environments in which actors operate (Sackmann, 1992; Adkins and Caldwell, 2004) and therefore also can serve a more micro context preserving role. Marketers are more like fellow marketers and share more norms, values, and language than they do with their organizational colleagues in manufacturing and operations, who in turn will differ from their colleagues in corporate finance. Naturally occurring experimentation tends to emerge and diffuse within these subgroups (Reagans and McEvily, 2003). At times this pattern has been viewed as a pathology, with knowledge remaining "sticky" (Szulanski, 1996). While certainly there may be important instances in which such patterns are indeed dysfunctional, this stickiness or localization of adoption may also reflect the degree to which contextualization is important.

7.1.4 Context-dependence and breadth of experimentation

Analogous to the tension between exploration and exploitation, we have a tension between the causal understanding and the wide range of possible interventions that random controlled trials offer, and therefore exploration-like possibilities, and the power of imitation from similar others, an exploitation-like process that does not require nor is even terribly supportive of causal understanding and can only offer up as possible candidates the set of existing practices and forms. Further, this contrast between RCTs and processes of possibly imperfect imitation or recombination is akin to the contrast with which this work started between classical conceptions of rational choice and Darwinian processes of descent with modification. Of course, the RCT suggests more modesty regarding the degree of a priori knowledge on the part of the strategists-experimenter than a standard rational approach. Not only is there an emphasis on learning, but there is not any claim that the optimal experiment is being run as in decision theoretic work on the design of experiments (DeGroot, 1970). In that regard, the RCT strategist-experimenter is much closer to our Mendel figure.

RCTs are Mendel-like in that they are acts of conscious experimentation. They do not rely on the presumed power of deductive reasoning in contrast to many classic approaches to strategy-making. However, the approach does not directly engage with either the issue of path-dependence or artificial selection—the dual pillars of the perspective developed here. The implicit assumption is that any experiment is possible, subject only to the imagination of the actors, and the evaluation is generally treated as unproblematic—a technical issue of statistical sampling. The consideration of path-dependence suggests that action may require more than imagination, but in addition some requisite set of capabilities. Further, this "imagination" is not independent of one's experiences (Gavetti and Menon, 2016).

In addition, the immediate consequence of an experimental trial is an interesting indicator of its possible value, but that indicator is both local in time and "space." That is, the performance measure is some measure of immediate feedback and that feedback is tied to the specific actor subject to the intervention. However, interventions may have non-local effects. For instance, a pay manipulation for actor i may have implications for the satisfaction and motivation of actor j based on social comparisons in which they may engage (Bandiera et al., 2010). Similarly, the near-term consequences of pricing and advertising interventions may differ significantly from their longer-term implications (Pauwels et al., 2002).

7.2 Design Implications

Figure 7.1 provides an overall perspective of the framework developed in this work. Two basic constructs are highlighted as influencing the dynamics of organizations: path-dependence and artificial selection. Path-dependence delineates the range of the "adjacent possible"; but, in the spirit of the active role of the Mendelian executive, there is tremendous discretion as to where within that range the organization might land. Artificial selection plays two distinct roles. The primary function of artificial selection is the mapping of market-level and other external outcome

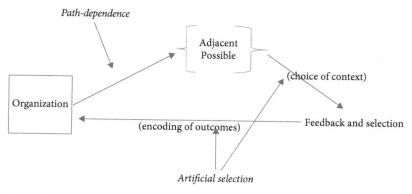

Figure 7.1 Dynamics of Organizational Adaptation.

measures to the culling and reinforcement of initiatives and actors within the organization. The second, higher-order consideration, is the choice of contexts in which the organization operates. The organization has no inherent mapping to a particular market niche and movement across distinct niches may result in quite different outcomes and feedback signals.

With this framework in mind, three fundamental roles of the Mendelian executive can be identified.

Encouraging Adjacencies: Effective growth and renewal is not a question of identifying the best of all possible worlds, but of identifying ways in which the organization can leverage its existing strengths into new possibilities. Such efforts entail many elements including supporting the scanning of the set of latent possibilities and helping to broker the connection between existing skills and activities into these new possibilities. The discussion of speciation in Chapter 6 highlights how relatively modest the investments were that were associated with the development of what ultimately proved to be quite significant new technologies and businesses. However, those investments were not zero. Further, what is "adjacent" is far from self-evident. As the discussion of Abbott and Flatlands in Chapter 5 suggests there is an enormous set of potential gradients that an organization might climb; further, as noted the set of latent niches in which the organization might operate is typically highly variegated. Thus, the particular landscapes of functionality that the organization might climb from a given starting point is typically quite large, and of similar scope in latent variety is the set of uses to which this functionality might be applied. The Mendelian executive is not, in a direct sense, the answer to these challenges, but rather a crafter of an organizational culture and organizational structure that facilitate a robust and ongoing process of search and discovery. A few basic principles are suggested below that might inform such efforts.

Agnostic Selection: The term agnostic selection is used to highlight the importance of a challenging duality of engaging in rigorous internal selection to facilitate the weeding out of less promising paths and the amplification of more promising pathways, while at the same time having a large dose of humility as to what selection criteria might best be invoked. As highlighted in our discussion of selection, a fundamental role of the organization is to mediate between the selection forces of the overall economic environment and the particular projects, initiatives, and individuals within the organization.

This potential loose coupling between the immediate demands and signals from the current niches in which the organization operates and the selection criteria imposed on the various initiatives within the organization offers the possibility of multiple selection criteria or even the suppression of selection as a whole as in the case of slack search. But this loose coupling does not connote wisdom, but simply the possibility of distinct and possibly muted selection forces. Some individuals within the organization may have considerable reputational capital, which in turn may cause the organization to some degree to ignore contemporaneous indicators of the possible merit of their new efforts and rather to "bet" on the person (Bower, 1970; Kaplan et al, 2009). Relatedly, the organization may engage in what AI researchers refer to as model-based evaluation (Sutton and Barto, 1998) in which environmental cues of outcomes are either not present or not attended to and instead evaluation of merit is based on a model of beliefs as to what constitute superior pathways and intermediate outcomes.[5] Per the possibility of "betting" on an individual, there is the question of what beliefs should substitute for the immediate cues from the current focal niche in which the organization is operating. Letting others in the organization ideate and pursue new courses of action is one thing. Letting these efforts continue contrary to one's own assessment of merit is a different challenge.

One approach that can facilitate a "disciplined agnosticism" is not to impose a set of criteria on a new initiative, but rather to let those who are championing this initiative specify their own "model of

---

[5] In this regard, it is interesting to consider so-called "actor-critique" (Holland et al., 1986) models which, as noted in the appendix to Chapter 4, have a "Mendelian" quality to them. An assessment is made not merely on the basis of direct trials, but also on the basis of the actor's valuation function. Further, this valuation function itself evolves through experience within the particular context as well as across contexts, with the efficacy of that process being a function of the quality of categorization scheme by which contexts are encoded, a key element in the learning system.

beliefs" as to why a particular pathway might be viable and what constitute the relevant indicators of this viability. Such an approach, however, becomes particularly challenging when initial efforts suggest a "pivot" to different gradients of functionality and distinct market niches. The pivot requires the agnostic selector to entertain the triplet of beliefs of the reasonableness of the initial set of beliefs; and, at the same time, their now, ex post, less than desired properties; and, as the final element in the triplet, the plausibility of the new proposed pathway.

It is interesting to contrast how this re-contracting process might operate within the context of an established enterprise and a fledging "lean start-up" (Contigiani and Levinthal, 2019). As Gibbons and Henderson (2012) observe, such re-contracting requires a considerable degree of trust among the parties—in this case, trust about the good faith efforts to realize the potential of proposed initiatives and the talents and insights of the key actors. While "pivoting" has become a celebrated norm in the world of start-ups (Blank, 2003; Ries, 2011), it is a process that appears to have more difficulty gaining traction in more established enterprises. One important distinction between the two settings is the more modest size and greater transparency of actions and outcomes of a start-up versus a new initiative embedded in a larger organization. Another important distinction is the lack of parallelism in the context of a lean start-up as the approach emphasizes having a singular focus. This lack of parallelism implies that resources will either be reallocated via a "pivot" or the organization itself will terminate and resources will be reallocated through markets for capital and labor. In contrast, an established enterprise typically sustains a diverse set of initiatives, leaving the possibility of the repurposing of resources from one initiative to another. Parallel developmental pathways within the same organization allow for adaptation to occur via the culling and scaling of this population of initiatives within the organization. In the context of a lean start-up, a pivot is the sole mechanism for within-organizational adaptation.

Engaging Ecologies: While Donne famously observed that no man is an island, a similar sentiment can be applied to business enterprises. In particular, there is a long line of work on the importance of complements in an overall business model (Teece, 1986; Adner, 2012), as well as observations about the possibility and importance of organizations influencing their environment, whether in efforts to enhance legitimacy (Sine and Lee, 2009) or by influencing the regulatory structure within which organizations operate (Ahuja et al., 2018).

The Mendelian executive has a further challenge in that they need to explore ways in which linkages with different organizations may, through feedback and signals, guide both the development of capabilities and resources within the organization and suggest promising adjacent niches and application domains. The evaluation of the merit of engaging and potentially shaping different niches has the same challenges of assessing ex ante what might constitute useful actions and the ambiguity of the evaluation ex-post indicators of outcomes that the orchestration of internal actions poses. So, while the ecosystem in which the organization might operate provides a broader canvas for the Mendelian executive, the limitations of what constitutes more or less useful brush strokes remains.

John Gardner (1972) noted that our thinking about growth and decay is dominated by the image of a single lifespan, but he argues that "for an ever-renewing society the appropriate image is a total garden, a balanced aquarium or other ecological system. Some things are being born, other things are flourishing, still other things are dying—but the system lives on." Per Gardner's observation, entities that have a sustained lifespan are not themselves static. An individual might live to a ripe old age of 100, but their individual cells are replacing themselves at a rapid, ongoing rate. Organizations face a far greater challenge of not merely rejuvenating a fixed form, but allowing that form to evolve to both take advantage of new opportunities and to respond to changes in its current context. The Mendelian executive acts with humility with regard to their own insight about possible futures to foster an organization capable of such renewal, but at the same time the Mendelian executive does act and serves as a catalyst for creative action on the part the organization.

The engine of organizational adaptation is fueled by the set of initiatives, ideas, products, technologies, and the like percolating throughout the organization and some mechanism by which these "variants" are culled and amplified. The extant population of activities at one point in time is not independent of what that population looked like at an earlier time point—the property of path-dependence. Further, the bases of selection are clearly not history independent. Arguably the management field would benefit from a consideration of not just specific tools of intended rationality, but a more general framework with which to situate the challenge of intentionality and adaptation in extraordinary complex and changing environments. The dual mechanisms of path-dependence and artificial selection are promising candidates for that role.

Where does all this leave our Mendelian executive? While the term "guided evolution" has been introduced to suggest an evolutionary perspective of management (Lovas and Ghoshal, 2000), the modifier guided as it relates to the framework developed here is arguably misleading. Yes, the Mendelian executive plays a critical role in nurturing the organization to be an effective adaptive entity, but they must do so in the absence of necessarily having a clear or definitive point of view as to what constitutes desired pathways. To maintain the "gardening" or cultivating imagery, the task is not breeding a particular variety of roses to have a distinct coloration. Rather, it is to be a catalyst for an organization whose desired products and services are not clear a priori. The Mendelian executive is a catalyst and cultivator of possibly promising pathways to not fully knowable futures.

Bibliography

Abbott, E. (1884) *Flatland: A Romance of Many Dimensions*. Seely & Co: London.

Abernathy, W. and J. Utterback (1978) "Patterns of industrial innovation." *Technology Review*, 80: 41–47.

Adkins, B. and D. Caldwell (2004) "Firm or subgroup culture: where does fitting in matter most?" *Journal of Organizational Behavior*, 25(8): 969–78.

Adner, R. (2002) "When are technologies disruptive? A demand-based view of the emergence of competition." *Strategic Management Journal*, 667–88.

Adner, R. (2012) *The Wide Lens*. Penguin Press: New York.

Adner, R. (2017) "Ecosystems as structure: an actionable construct for strategy." *Journal of Management*, 43: 39–58.

Adner, R. and D. A. Levinthal (2002) "The emergence of emerging technologies." *California Management Review*, 45(1): 50–66.

Adner, R. and D. Levinthal (2004) "Real options and real tradeoffs." *Academy of Management Review*, 29: 120–6.

Adner, R. and D. Levinthal (2008) "Doing versus seeing: acts of exploitation and perceptions of exploration. *Strategic Entrepreneurship Journal*, 2: 43–52.

Adner, R. and P. Zemsky (2005) "Disruptive technologies and the emergence of competition." *Rand Journal*, 36(2): 229–54.

Ahuja, G., L. Capron, M. Lenox, and D. Yao (2018) "Strategy and the institutional envelope." *Strategy Science*, 3(2): ii–x.

Alchian, A. and H. Demsetz (1972) "Production, information cost and economic organization." *American Economic Review*, 62(5): 777–95.

Aldrich, H. (1999) *Organizations Evolving*. Sage Publications: London.

Amram, M. and N. Kulatilaka (1999) *Real Options: Managing Strategic Investment in an Uncertain World*. Harvard Business School Press: Boston.

Anderson, P. and M. Tushman (1990) "Technological discontinuities and dominant designs: a cyclical model of technological change." *Administrative Science Quarterly*, 35(4): 604–33.

Andrews, K. (1971) *The Concept of Corporate Strategy*. Dow-Jones Irwin: Homewood, IL.

Argote, L. (1999) *Organizational Learning: Creating, Retaining and Transferring Knowledge*. Kluwer: Norwell, MA.

Argyris, C. and D. Schon (1974) *Theory in Practice*. Jossey-Bass: San Francisco.

Arthur, B. (1989) "Competing technologies, increasing returns, and lock-in by historical events." *Economic Journal*, 99: 116–31.

Arthur, W. (2002) "The emerging conceptual framework of evolutional developmental biology." *Nature*, 415(14): 757–64.

Athey, S. and G. Imbens (2016) "Recursive partitioning for heterogeneous causal effects." *PNAS*, 113(27): 7353–60.

Baldwin, C. (2007) "Where do transactions come from? Modularity, transactions, and the boundaries of firms." *Industrial and Corporate Change*, 17(1): 155–95.

Baldwin, C. and K. Clark (2000) *Design Rules: The Power of Modularity*. MIT Press: Cambridge, MA.

Bandiera, O., I. Barankay, and I. Rasul (2010) "Social incentives in the workplace." *Review of Economic Studies*, 77(2): 417–58.

Barnett, W. (2008) *The Red Queen among Organizations*. Princeton University Press: Princeton.

Barney, J. (1986) "Strategic factor market: expectations, luck, and business strategy." *Management Science*, 32(10): 1231–41.

Barney, J. (1991) "Firm resources and sustained competitive advantage." *Journal of Management*, 17(1): 99–120.

Baron, J., D. Burton, and M. Hannan (1996) "The road taken: origins and evolution of employment systems in emerging companies." *Industrial and Corporate Change*, 5: 239–75.

Barron, D., E. West, and M. Hannan (1994) "A time to grow and a time to die: growth and mortality of credit units in New York City, 1914–1990." *American Journal of Sociology*, 100: 381–421.

Barton, N. and B. Charlesworth (1998) "Why sex and recombination?" *Science*, 281: 1986–90.

Basalla, G. 1988. *The Evolution of Technology*. Cambridge University Press: New York.

Battilana, J. and M. Lee (2014) "Advancing research on hybrid organizing: insights from the study of social enterprises." *Academy of Management Annals*, 8: 397–441.

Baumann, O., J. Schmidt, and N. Stieglitz (2019) "Effective search in rugged performance landscapes." *Journal of Management*, 45(1): 285–318.

Beckman, C. and M. Burton (2008) "Founding the future: path dependence in the evolution of top management teams from founding to IPO." *Organization Science*, 19: 3–24.

Bellman, R. (1957) *Dynamic Programming*. Princeton University Press: Princeton.

Bellman, R. (1961) *Adaptive Control Processes: A Guided Tour*. Princeton University Press: Princeton.

Benner, M. and R. Ranganathan (2013) "Divergent reaction to convergent strategies: Investor beliefs and analysts reactions during technological change". *Organization Science*, 24(2): 378-394.

Berger, P. and T. Luckmann (1967) *The Social Construction of Reality*. Anchor Books: New York.

Berry, D. and B. Fristedt (1985) *Bandit Problems: Sequential Allocation of Experiments*. Chapman and Hall: London.

Birnholtz, J., M. Cohen, and V. Susannah (2007) "Organizational character: on the regeneration of Camp Popular Grove." *Organization Science*, 18(2): 315–32.

Blank, S. (2003) *The Four Steps to the Epiphany: Successful Strategies for Products That Win*. CafePress: Foster City, CA.

Bloch F., E. C. Levinthal, and M. E. Packard (1947) "Relative nuclear moments of H1 and H2." *Physics Review*, 72: 1125–6.

Block, Z. and I. MacMillan (1993) *Corporate Venturing: Creating New Businesses within the Firm*. Harvard Business School Press: Boston.

Bloom, N., E. Benn, A. Mahajan, D. McKenzie, and J. Roberts (2013) "Does management matter: evidence from India." *Quarterly Journal of Economics*, 128(1): 1–51.

Boisnier, A. and J. A. Chatman (2003) "The role of subcultures in agile organizations." In *Leading and Managing People in Dynamic Organizations*, ed. R. Peterson and E. Mannix, pp. 87–112. Earlbaum: Mahwah, NJ.

Bower, J. (1970) *Managing the Resource Allocation Process*. Harvard Business School Press: Boston.

Bowman, E. H. and G. T. Moskowitz (2001) "Real options analysis and strategic decision making." *Organization Science*, 12: 772–7.

Bradach, J. (1997) "Using the plural form in the management of restaurant chains." *Administrative Science Quarterly*, 42: 276–303.

Brittain, J. and J. Freeman (1980) "Organizational proliferation and density dependent selection." In *The Organizational Life-Cycle*, ed. J. Kimberly and R. Miles, pp. 291–341. Jossey-Bass: San Francisco.

Brown, T. (2009) *Change by Design: How Design Thinking Transforms Organizations and Inspires Innovation*. HarperCollins: New York.

Burgelman, R. (1991) "Intraorganizational ecology of strategy making and organizational adaptation: theory and field research." *Organization Science*, 2: 239–62.

Burgelman, R. (1994) "Fading memories: a process theory of strategic business exit in dynamic competitive environments." *Administrative Science Quarterly*, 39: 24–56.

Campbell, D. T. (1965) "Variation and selective retention in sociocultural evolution." In *Social Change in Developing Areas: A Reinterpretation of Evolutionary Theory*, ed. H. R. Barringer, G. I. Blanksten, and R. W. Mack, pp. 19–49. Schenkman: Cambridge, MA.

Carroll, G. and A. Swaminathan (2000) "Why the microbrewery movement? Organizational dynamics of resource partitioning in the U.S. brewing industry." *American Journal of Sociology*, 106(3): 715–62.

Cattani, G. (2005) "Pre-adaptation, firm heterogeneity and technological performance: a study on the evolution of fiber optics, 1970–1995." *Organization Science*, 16(6): 563–80.

Cattani, G. and D. Levinthal (2005) "Reconciling phyletic gradualism with punctuated equilibrium: an integrated view of evolutionary change." Unpublished memo.

Chesbrough, H. (2002) "Graceful exits and foregone opportunities: Xerox's management of its technology spinoff organizations." *Business History Review*, 76(4): 803–38.

Christensen, C. (1997) *The Innovator's Dilemma*. Harvard University Press: Cambridge, MA.

Christensen, C. and R. Rosenbloom (1995) "Explaining the attractors advantage and technological paradigms, organizational dynamics, and the value network." *Research Policy*, 24: 237–57.

Christensen, M. and T. Knudsen (2010) "Design of decision-making organizations." *Management Science*, 56(1): 71–89.

Coase, R. (1937) "The nature of the firm." *Economica*, 4(16): 386–405.

Cohen, W. and D. Levinthal (1989) "Innovation and learning: the two faces of r&d." *Economic Journal*, 99: 569–96.

Cohen, W. and D. Levinthal (1990) "Absorptive capacity: a new perspective on learning and innovation." *Administrative Science Quarterly*, 35: 128–52.

Cohen, W. and D. Levinthal (1994) "Fortune favors the prepared firm." *Management Science*, 40: 227–51.

Cohen, M. D., J. G. March, and J. P. Olsen (1972) "A garbage can model of organizational change." *Administrative Science Quarterly*, 17: 1–25.

Contigiani, A. and D. Levinthal (2019) "Situating the construct of lean start-up: adjacent conversations and possible future directions." *Industrial and Corporate Change*, 28: 551–64.

Csaszar, F. (2013) "An efficient frontier in organizational design: organizational structure as a determinant of exploration and exploitation." *Organization Science*, 24(4): 1083–1101.

Csaszar, F. and D. Levinthal (2016) "Mental representation and the discovery of new strategies." *Strategic Management Journal*, 37: 2013–49.

Cyert, R. and J. March (1963) *A Behavioral Theory of the Firm*. Prentice-Hall: Englewood, NJ.

D'Aveni, R. (1994) *Hypercompetition*. Free Press: New York.

Darwin, Charles (1859) *On the Origin of the Species by Means of Natural Selection*. Murray: London.

David, P. (1985) "Clio and the economics of QWERTY." *American Economic Review*, 75(2): 332–7.

Dawkins, R. (1987) *The Blind Watchmaker*. W. W. Norton: New York.

DeGroot, M. (1970) *Optimal Statistical Decisions*. McGraw-Hill: New York.

Dennett, D. (1991) *Consciousness Explained*. Little Brown: Boston.

Dennett, D. (1995) *Darwin's Dangerous Idea*. Simon & Schuster: New York.

Denrell, J., C. Fang, and D. Levinthal (2004) "From T-mazes to labyrinths: learning from model-based feedback." *Management Science*, 50: 1366–78.

Denrell, J. and J. March (2001) "Adaptation as information restriction: the hot stove effect." *Organization Science*, 12(5): 523–38.

Dierickx, I. and K. Cool (1989) "Asset stock accumulation and sustainability of competitive advantage." *Management Science*, 35: 1504–11.

Dosi, G. (1983) "Technological paradigms and technological trajectories." *Research Policy*, 11: 147–62.

Dushnitsky, G. and M. Lenox (2005) "When do firms undertake R&D by investing in new ventures?" *Strategic Management Journal*, 26: 947–65.

Dushnitsky, G. and Z. Shapira (2010) "Entrepreneurial finance meets organizational reality: comparing investment practices and performance of corporate and independent venture capitalists." *Strategic Management Journal*, 31: 990–1017.

Eisenhardt, K. and J. Martin (2000) "Dynamic capabilities: what are they?" *Strategic Management Journal*, 21: 1105–21.

Eldredge, N. and S. J. Gould (1972) "Punctuated equilibria: an alternative to phyletic gradualism." In *Models in Paleobiology*, ed. T. J. M. Schopf, pp. 82–115. Freeman, Cooper and Co.: San Francisco.

Elfwing, S., E. Uchibe, K. Doya, and H. Christensen (2008) "Co-evolution of shaping rewards and meta-parameters in reinforcement learning." *Adaptive Behavior*, 16: 400–12.

Ethiraj, S. (2007) "Allocation of inventive effort in complex product systems." *Strategic Management Journal*, 28: 563–84.

Ethiraj, S. and D. Levinthal (2004) "Modularity and innovation in complex systems." *Management Science*, 50(2): 159–73.

Ethiraj, S. and D. Levinthal (2009) "Hoping for A to Z while rewarding only A: complex organizations and multiple goals." *Organization Science*, 20: 4–24.

Feigenbaum, E. (1978) "The art of artificial intelligence: themes and case studies." *AFIPS Conference Proceeding*, 47: 227.

Feldman M. and B. Pentland (2003) "Reconceptualizing organizational routines as a source of flexibility and change." *Administrative Science Quarterly*, 48(1): 94–118.

Fleming, L. (2001) "Recombinant uncertainty in technological search." *Management Science*, 47(1): 117–32.

Fligstein, N. (1985) "The spread of the multidivisional form among large firms, 1919–1979." *American Sociological Review*, 50: 377–91.

Freeland, R. and E. Zuckerman Sivan (2018) "The problems and promise of hierarchy: voice rights and the firm." *Sociological Science*, 5: 143–81.

Fudenberg, D. and J. Tirole (1988) *The Theory of Industrial Organization*. MIT Press: Cambridge, MA.

Ganz, S. (2018) "Ignorant decision making and educated inertia: some political pathologies of organizational learning." *Organization Science*, 29(1): 39–57.

Gärdenfors P. (2000) *Conceptual Spaces: The Geometry of Thought*. MIT Press: Cambridge, MA.

Gardner, J. (1972) *In Common Cause*. W. W. Norton: New York.

Gavetti, G. (2012) "Toward a behavioral theory of strategy." *Organization Science*, 23(1): 267–85.

Gavetti, G., C. Helfat, and L. Marengo (2017) "Searching, shaping, and the quest for superior performance." *Strategy Science*, 2(3): 194–209.

Gavetti, G. and D. Levinthal (2000) "Looking forward and looking backward: cognitive and experiential search," *Administrative Science Quarterly*, 45: 113–37.

Gavetti, G., D. Levinthal, and W. Ocasio (2007) "Neo-Carnegie: the Carnegie School's past, present, and reconstructing for the future." *Organizational Science*, 18: 523–36.

Gavetti, G., D. A. Levinthal, and J. W. Rivkin (2005) "Strategy making in novel and complex worlds: the power of analogy." *Strategic Management Journal*, 26(8): 691–712.

Gavetti, G. and A. Menon (2016) "Evolution cum agency: toward a model of strategic foresight." *Strategy Science*, 1(3): 207–33.

Gersick, C. J. G. (1988) "Time and transition in work teams." *Academy of Management Journal*, 31: 10–36.

Gersick, C. J. G. (1991) "Revolutionary change theories: a multilevel exploration of the punctuated equilibrium paradigm." *Academy of Management Journal*, 16(1): 10–36.

Ghemawat, P. (2002) "Competition and business strategy in historical perspective." *Business History Review*, 76(1): 37–74.

Gibbons, R. (1999) "Taking Coase seriously." *Administrative Science Quarterly*, 44(1): 145–57.

Gibbons, R. and R. Henderson (2012) "Relational contracts and organizational capabilities." *Organization Science*, 23(5): 1350–64.

Gibbons, R. and J. Roberts (2013) *Handbook of Organizational Economics*. Princeton University Press: Princeton.

Gittins, J. C. (1979) "Bandit processes and dynamic allocation indices." *Journal of the Royal Statistical Society*, Series B Methodological, 41(2): 148–77.

Goldschmidt, R. B. (1940) *The Material Basis of Evolution*. Yale University Press: New Haven.

Gould, S. J. (1980) *The Panda's Thumb*. W. W. Norton: New York.

Gould, S. J. and N. Eldridge (1977) "Punctuated equilibria: the tempo and mode of evolution reconsidered." *Paleobiology*, 3: 115–51.

Gould, S. J. and R. Lewontin (1979) "The spandrels of San Marco and the Panglossian paradigm: a critique of the adaptationist programme." *Proceedings of the Royal Society of London. Series B, Biological Sciences*, 205: 581–98.

Gould, S. J. and E. S. Vrba (1982) "Exaptation: a missing term in the science of form." *Paleobiology*, 8: 4–15.

Greiner, L. (1972) "Evolution and revolution as organizations grow." *Harvard Business Review*, 50(4): 37–46.

Guler, I. (2018) "Pulling the plug: the capability to terminate unsuccessful projects and firm performance." *Strategy Science*, 3: 481–97.

Greve, H. (2003) *Organizational Learning from Performance Feedback*. Cambridge University Press: Cambridge.

Gurley, W. (1999) "The rising importance of the great art of story telling." *Above the Crowd*. Available at cnetnews.com. October 18, 1999.

Gwyne, P. (1997) "Skunk works—1990s style." *Research & Technology Mangaement*, 40(4): 18–23.

Halford, G., W. Wilson, J. Guo, W. Gayler, J. Wiles, and J. Stewart (1994) "Connectionist implications for processing capacity limitations in analogies." In *Advances in Connectionist and Neural Computation Theory, Vol. 2. Analogical Connections*, ed. K. Holyoak and J. Barnden, pp. 363–415. Ablex: Norwood, NJ.

Hall, B., B. Pearson, and G. Müller. (2003) *Environment, Development, and Evolution*. MIT Press: Cambridge, MA.

Hannan, M. and J. Freeman (1984) "Structural inertia and organizational change." *American Sociological Review*, 82: 149–64.

Hannigan, T., R. Haans, K. Vakili, H. Tschalian, V. Glaser, S. Kaplan, and P. D. Jennings (2019) "Topic modeling in management research." *Academy of Management Annals*, 13: 586–632.

Hargadon, A. and R. Sutton (1997) "Technology brokering and innovation in a product development firm". *Administrative Science Quarterly*, 42(4): 716–49.

Hawk, A., G. Pacheco de Almeida, and B. Yeung (2013) "Fast-mover advantages: speed capabilities and entry into the emerging submarket of Atlantic Basin LNG. *Strategic Management Journal*, 34(13): 1531–50.

Helfat, C., S. Finkelstein, W. Mitchell, M. Peteraf, H. Singh, D. Teece, and S. Winter (2007) *Dynamic Capabilities*. Blackwell Publishing: Oxford.

Henderson, R. and K. Clark (1990) "Architectural innovation: the reconfiguration of existing product technologies and the failure of established firms." *Administrative Science Quarterly*, 35: 9–30.

Henig, R. M. (2001) *The Monk in the Garden*. Mariner Books: New York.

Hodgson, G. and T. Knudsen (2010) *Darwin's Conjecture: The Search for General Principles of Social and Economic Evolution*. University of Chicago Press: Chicago.

Holland, J. (1975) *Adaptation in Natural and Artificial Systems: An Introductory Analysis with Applications in Biology, Control & Artificial Intelligence*. University of Michigan Press: Ann Arbor.

Holland, J., K. Holyoak, R. Nisbett, and P. Thagard (1986) *Induction: Processes of Inference, Learning, and Discovery*. MIT Press: Cambridge, MA.

Holmstrom, B. (2017) "Pay for performance and beyond." *American Economic Review*, 197(7): 1753–77.

Holyoak, K. and P. Thagard (1995) *Mental Leaps: Analogy in Creative Thought*. MIT Press: Cambridge, MA.

Hrebeniak, L. and W. Joyce (1985) "Organizational adaptation: strategic choice and environmental determinism." *Administrative Science Quarterly*, 30: 336–45.

Hsu, G. and M. Hannan (2005) "Identities, genres, and organizational forms." *Organization Science*, 16(5): 474–90.

Iyer, B. and T. H. Davenport (2008) "Reverse engineering Google's innovation machine" *Harvard Business Review*, 86(4): 58–68.

Jacobides, M. G., T. Knudsen, and M. Augier (2006) "Benefiting from innovation: value creation, value appropriation and the role of industry architectures." *Research Policy*, 35: 1200–21.

Jermier, J. M., J. W. Slocum, Jr, L. W. Fry, and J. Gaines (1991) "Organizational subcultures in a soft bureaucracy: resistance behind the myth and facade of an official culture." *Organization Science*, 2(2): 170–94.

Joseph, J. and V. Gaba (2014) "The fog of feedback: ambiguity and firm-responses to multiple aspiration levels." *Strategic Management Journal*, 36: 1960–78.

Joseph, J. and W. Ocasio (2012) "Architecture, attention, and adaptation in the multibusiness firm: General Electric from 1951 to 2001." *Strategic Management Journal*, 33: 633–60.

Kale, P. and H. Singh (2007) "Building firm capabilities through learning: the role of alliance learning process in alliance capability and firm-level alliance success." *Strategic Management Journal*, 28: 981–1000.

Kanter, R. M. (1988) "When a thousand flowers bloom." *Research in Organizational Behavior*, 10: 169–211.

Kaplan, S. (2008) "Framing contests: strategy making under uncertainty." *Organization Science*, 19(5): 729–52.

Kaplan, S. N., B. A. Sensoy, and P. Strömberg (2009) "Should investors bet on the jockey or the horse? Evidence from the evolution of firms from early business plans to public companies". *The Journal of Finance*, 64(1): 75–115.

Kauffman, S. (2000) *Investigations*. Oxford University Press: Oxford.

Kauffman, S. and S. Levins (1987) "Toward a general theory of adaptive walks on rugged landscapes." *Journal of Theoretical Biology*, 128: 11–45.

Kimberly, J. and R. Miles (1981) *The Organization Life Cycle*. Jossey-Bass: San Francisco.

Kingdon, J. (1984) *Agendas, Alternatives, and Public Policy*. HarperCollins: New York.

Kleinbaum, A., T. Stuart, and M. Tushman (2013) "Discretion within constraint: homophily and structure in a formal organization." *Organization Science*, 24(5): 1316–36.

Klepper S. (1996) "Entry, exit, growth and innovation over the product life cycle." *American Economic Review*, 86(3): 562–83.

Klepper, S. and P. Thompson (2010) "Disagreements and intra-industry spinoffs." *International Journal of Industrial Organization*, 28(5): 526–38.

Knight, F. (1921) *Risk, Uncertainty, and Profit*. Houghton Mifflin: Boston.

Knudsen, T. and G. Hodgson (2010) *Darwin's Conjecture*. University of Chicago Press: Chicago.

Knudsen, T. and D. Levinthal (2007) "Two faces of search: alternative generation and alternative evaluation." *Organizational Science*, 18: 39–54.

Kohavi, R. and R. Longbotham (2017). "Online controlled experiment and a/b testing." In Encyclopedia of Machine Learning and Data Mining Ed. C. Sammut and G. Webb. Springer: New York.

Krizhevsky, A., L. Sutskever, and G. Hinton (2012) "ImageNet classification with deep convolutional neural networks." *Proceedings of the 25th International Conference on Neural Information Processing Systems*, pp. 1097–1105.

Lansing, S. (1987) "'Water temples' and the management of irrigation." *American Anthropologist*, 89: 326–41.

Lave, C. and J. G. March (1975) *An Introduction to Models in the Social Sciences*. Harper & Row: New York.

Lavie, D., J. Kang, and L. Rosenkopf (2011) "Balance within and across domains: the performance implications of exploration and exploitation in alliances." *Organization Science*, 22(6): 1517–38.

Leiblein, M., J. Reuer, and T. Zenger (2018) "What makes a decision strategic?" *Strategy Science*, 3: 555–73.

Leonard-Barton, D. (1992) "Core capabilities and core rigidities: a paradox in managing new product development." *Strategic Management Journal*, 13: 111–25.

Levine, J. M. and R. Moreland (1991) "Culture and socialization in work groups." In *Perspectives on Socially Shared Cognition*, ed. L. B. Resnick, J. M. Levine, and S. D. Teasley, pp. 257–79. American Psychological Association: Washington, D.C.

Levinthal, D. (1991a) "Organizational adaptation and environmental selection: interrelated processes of change." *Organizational Science*, 2: 140–5.

Levinthal, D. (1991b) "Random walks and organizational mortality." *Administrative Science Quarterly*, 36: 397–420.

Levinthal, D. (1997) "Adaptation on Rugged Landscapes." *Management Science*, 43: 934–50.

Levinthal, D. (1998) "The slow pace of rapid technological change: gradualism and punctuation in technological knowledge." *Industrial and Corporate Change*, 7(2): 217–47.

Levinthal, D. (2000) "Organizational capabilities in complex worlds." In *The Nature and Dynamics of Organizational Capabilities*, ed. G. Dosi, R. Nelson, and S. Winter, pp. 364–80. Oxford University Press: Oxford.

Levinthal, D. (2002) "Cognition and models of adaptive learning." in *Economics of Change, Choice, and Structure: Essays in the Memory of Richard M. Cyert*, ed. J. March and M. Augier. Edward Elgar Publishing, Ltd.: Cheltonham.

Levinthal, D. (2011) "A behavioral approach to strategy: what's the alternative?" *Strategic Management Review*, 32: 1517–24.

Levinthal, D. (2017) "Resource allocation and firm boundaries." *Journal of Management*, 43(8): 2580–7.

Levinthal, D. and J. March (1993) "The myopia of learning." *Strategic Management Journal*, 14: 95–112.

Levinthal, D. and A. Marino (2015) "Three facets of organizational adaptation: selection, variety, and plasticity." *Organization Science*, 26(3): 743–55.

Levinthal, D. and H. Posen (2007) "Myopia of selection: does organizational adaptation limit the efficacy of population selection?" *Administrative Science Quarterly*, 52: 586–620.

Levinthal, D. and C. Rerup (forthcoming) "The plural of goal: learning in a world of ambiguity." *Organization Science*.

Levinthal, D. and M. Warglien (1999) "Landscape design: designing for local action in complex worlds." *Organization Science*, 10: 342–57.

Levinthal, D. and B. Wu (2010) "The rational tradeoff between corporate scope and profit margins: the role of capacity-constrained capabilities and market maturity." *Strategic Management Journal*, 31: 780–801.

Levitt, B. and J. G. March (1988) "Organizational learning." *Annual Review of Sociology*, 14: 319–40.

Lewis, C. S. (2005) *The Magician's Nephew*. HarperCollins: New York.

Lichtenstein, B. M. (1995) "Evolution or transformation: a critique and alternative to punctuated equilibrium." *Academy of Management Proceedings*, 1: 291–8.

Lovas, B. and S. Ghoshal (2000) "Strategy as guided evolution." *Strategic Management Journal*, 21(9): 875–96.

Luce, R. 1959. *Individual Choice Behavior: A Theoretical Analysis*. Wiley: New York.

March, J. (1962) "The firm as a political coalition." *American Political Science Review*, 24(4): 162–78.

March, J. G. (1991) "Exploration and exploitation in organizational learning." *Organization Science*, 2: 71–87.

March, J. G., L. Sproul, and M. Tamuz (1991). "Learning from samples of one or fewer". *Organization Science*, 2: 1–13.

March, J. G. (1994) *A Primer on Decision-Making*. Free Press: New York.

March, J. G. (2006) "Rationality, foolishness, and adaptive intelligence." *Strategic Management Journal*, 27: 201–14.

March, J. G. and J. P. Olsen (1984) "The new institutionalism: organizational factors in political life." *American Political Science Review*, 78: 734–49.

March, J. G. and H. Simon (1958) *Organizations*. Wiley: New York.

March, J. G., L. Sproul, and M. Tamuz (1991) "Learning from samples of one or fewer." *Organization Science*, 2: 1–13.

Mayr, E. (1988) *Toward a New Philosophy of Biology: Observations of an Evolutionist*. Harvard University Press: Cambridge, MA.

McGahan, A. and M. Porter (1997) "How much does industry matter, really?" *Strategic Management Journal*, 18: 15–30.

McGrath, R. G. (1997) "A real options logic for initiating technology positioning investments." *Academy of Management Review*, 22: 974–96.

Michels, R. (1915) *Political Parties*. Hearst Library Co.: New York.

Miller, D. and P. H. Friesen (1980) "Momentum and revolution in organizational adaptation." *Academy of Management Journal*, 23(4): 591–614.

Miner, A. and P. Haunschild (1995) "Population level learning." In *Research in Organizational Behavior*, ed. L. L. Cummings and B. M. Staw, pp. 115–66. JAI Press: Greenwich, CT.

Minsky, M. (1961) "Steps toward artificial intelligence." *Proceedings of the IRE*, 49(1): 8–30.

Mokyr, J. (1990) "Punctuated equilibria and technological progress." *The American Economic Review*, 80(2): 350–4.

Mokyr, J. (1991) "Evolutionary biology, technological change and economic history." *Bulletin of Economic Research*, 43(2): 127–49.

Myer, J. and B. Rowan (1977) "Institutionalizing organizations: formal structures as myth and ceremony." *American Journal of Sociology*, 83: 340–63.

Nelson, R. (1961) "Uncertainty, learning, and the economics of parallel research and development." *Review of Economics and Statistics*, 43: 351–68.

Nelson R. and S. Winter (1982) *An Evolutionary Theory of Economic Change*. Belknap Press: Cambridge, MA.

Newel, A. and H. Simon (1972) *Human Problem Solving*. Prentice-Hall: Englewood, NJ.

Nickerson, J. and T. Zenger (2002) "Being efficiently fickle: a dynamic theory of organizational choice." *Organization Science*, 13(5): 547–66.

Obloj, T. and M. Sengul (2020) "What do multiple objectives really mean for performance? Empirical evidence from the French manufacturing sector." *Strategic Management Journal*, 41(13): 2518–47.

Odling-Smee, F. J. (2003) *Niche Construction: The Neglected Process in Evolution*. Princeton University Press: Princeton.

Osborn, A. (1953) *Applied Imagination: Principals and Procedures of Creative Thinking*. Scribner: New York.

Ouchi, W. (1980) "Markets, bureaucracies, and clans." *Administrative Science Quarterly*, 25: 129–41.

Page, S. (2007) *The Difference: How the Power of Diversity Makes Better Groups, Organizations, Schools, and Societies*. Princeton University Press: Princeton.

Pauwels, K., D. M. Hanssens, and S. Siddarth (2002) "The long-term effects of price promotions on category incidence, brand choice, and purchase quantity." *Journal of Marketing Research*, 39(4): 421–39.

Penrose, E. (1959) *The Theory of the Growth of the Firm*. M. E. Sharpe: White Plains, NY.

Phillips, D. (2011) "Jazz and the disconnected: city structural disconnectedness and the emergence of a jazz canon, 1897–1933." *American Journal of Sociology*, 117: 420–83.

Pigliucci, M. (2001) *Phenotypic Plasticity: Beyond Nature and Nurture*. Johns Hopkins University Press: Baltimore.

Polanyi, M. (1964) *Personal Knowledge*. Harper & Row: New York.

Pontikes, E. (2018) "Category strategy for firm advantage." *Strategy Science*, 3(4): 620–31.

Pontikes, E. and V. Rindova (2020) "Strategy making through temporal, constructive, and interactive agency." *Strategy Science*, 5(3): 149–59.

Porter, M. (1990) *The Competitive Advantage of Nations*. Free Press: New York.

Porter, M. (1996) "What is strategy?" *Harvard Business Review*, 74: 61–78.

Posen, H., J. Lee and Sangyoon Yi (2013) "The power of imperfect imitation." *Strategic Management Journal*, 34: 149–64.

Posen, H. and D. Levinthal (2012) "Chasing a moving target: exploration and exploitation in a dynamic environment." *Management Science*, 58: 587–601.

Prahalad, C. and R. Bettis (1986) "The dominant logic: a new linkage between diversity and performance." *Strategic Management Journal*, 7: 485–501.

Puranam, P. (2018) *The Microstructure of Organizations*. Oxford University Press: Oxford.

Puranam, P. and B. Vanneste (2016) *Corporate Strategy: Tools for Analysis and Decision Making*. Cambridge University Press: Cambridge.

Ranganathan, R. and L. Rosenkopf (2014) "Do ties really bind? The effect of knowledge and commercialization networks on opposition to standards." *Academy of Management Journal*, 57(2): 515–40.

Rao, H., P. Monin, and R. Durand (2005) "Boundary crossing: bricoloage and the erosion of categorical boundaries in French gastronomy." *American Sociological Review*, 70(6): 968–91.

Reagans, R. and B. McEvily (2003) "Network structure and knowledge transfer: the effects of cohesion." *Administrative Science Quarterly*, 48(2): 240–67.

Reich, L. S. (1985) *The Making of American Industrial Research. Science and Business at GE and Bell, 1876–1926*. Cambridge University Press: New York.

Ries, E. (2011) *The Lean Startup: How Today's Entrepreneurs Use Continuous Innovation to Create Radically Successful Businesses*. Crown Business: New York.

Rivkin, J. (2000) "Imitation of complex strategies." *Management Science*, 46(4): 824–44.

Rivkin, J. and N. Siggelkow (2003) "Balancing search and stability: interdependencies among elements of organizational design." *Management Science*, 49(3): 290–311.

Romanelli, E. and M. L. Tushman (1994) "Organizational transformation as punctuated equilibrium: an empirical test." *Academy of Management Journal*, 37(5): 1141–66.

Rosenberg, N. (1963) "Technological change in the machine tool industry: 1840–1910." *Journal of Economic History*, 23(4): 414–43.

Rumelhart, D. and J. McClelland (1986) *Parallel Decision Processes: Explorations in the Microstructure of Cognition*. MIT Press: Cambridge, MA.

Rumelt, R. P. (1991) "How much does industry matter?" *Strategic Management Journal*, 12(3): 167–85.

Sackmann, S. A. (1992) "Culture and subcultures: an analysis of organizational knowledge." *Administrative Science Quarterly*, 37(1): 140–61.

Sah, R. and J. Stiglitz (1988) "The architecture of economic systems: hierarchies and polyarchies." *American Economic Review*, 76(4): 716–27.

Samuel, A. (1959) "Some studies in machine learning using the game of checkers." *IBM Journal of Research and Development*, 31: 211–29.

Samuel, A. (1967) "Some studies in machine learning using the game of checkers II: recent progress." *IBM Journal of Research and Development*, 11: 601–17.

Samuelson, P. (1947) *Foundations of Economic Analysis*. Harvard University Press: Cambridge, MA.

Santos, F. and K. Eisenhardt (2009) "Constructing markets and shaping boundaries: entrepreneurial power in nascent fields." *Academy of Management Journal*, 52(4): 643–71.

Savage, L. (1954) *The Foundations of Statistics*. Wiley: New York.

Schaffer, C. (1993) "Overfitting avoidance as bias." *Machine Learning*, 10(2): 153–78.

Schumpeter, J. A. (1934) *The Theory of Economic Development*. Harvard University Press: Cambridge, MA.

Schilling, M. (2000) "Toward a general modular systems theory and its application to interfirm product modularity." *Academy of Management Review*, 25(2): 312–34.

Selton, R. (1975) "Reexamination of the perfectness concept for equilibrium points in extensive form games." *International Journal of Game Theory*, 4: 25–55.

Shaver, M. (1998) "Accounting for endogeneity when assessing strategy performance: does entry mode choice effect FDI survival?". *Management Science*, 44(4): 571–85.

Shin, J. and K. Milkman (2016) "How backup plans can harm goal pursuit: the unexpected downside of being prepared for failure." *Organizational Behavior and Human Decision Processes*, 135: 1–9.

Siggelkow, N. (2001) "Change in the persistence of fit: the rise, the fall, and the renaissance of Liz Claiborne." *Academy of Management Journal*, 44(4): 838–57.

Siggelkow, N. and D. Levinthal (2004) "Temporally divide to conquer: centralized, decentralized, and reintegrated organizational adaptations to exploration and adaptation." *Organization Science*, 14: 650–69.

Siggelkow, N. and D. Levinthal (2005) "Escaping real (non-benign) competency traps: linking the dynamics of the organizational structure to the dynamics of search." *Strategic Organization*, 3: 85–115.

Simon, H. (1962) "The architecture of complexity." *Proceedings of the American Philosophical Society*, 106: 467–82.

Simon, H. A. (1955) "A behavioral model of rational choice." *Quarterly Journal of Economics*, 69(1): 99–110.

Simon, H. A. (1976 [1947]) *Administrative Behavior: A Study of Decision-Making Processes in Administrative Organization*. Free Press: New York.

Sine, W. and B. Lee (2009) "Tilting at windmills? The environmental movement and the emergence of the U.S. wind energy sector." *Administrative Science Quarterly*, 54(1): 123–55.

Singh, S., R. Lewis, A. Barto, and J. Sorg (2010) "Intrinsically motivated reinforcement learning: An evolutionary perspective." *IEEE Transactions on Autonomous Mental Development*, 2(2): 70–82.

Skinner, B. (1957) *Verbal Behavior*. Appleton-Century-Crofts: New York.

Smith, A. (1776) *The Wealth of Nations*. Strahan and Cadell: London.

Sontag, S. (2002) "An argument about beauty." *Daedalus*, 131(4): 21–6.

Sorenson, O. and J. Sørensen (2001) "Finding the right mix: Franchising, organizational learning, and chain performance." *Strategic Management Journal*, 22: 713–24.

Stebbins, L. G. and F. Ayala (1981) "Is a new synthesis necessary?" *Science*, 213(28): 967–71.

Stein, J. (2003) "Agency, information, and corporate investment." In *Handbook of the Economics of Finance*, ed. G.M. Constantinides, M. Harris, and R. Stulz, pp. 113–65. Elsevier Science: Amsterdam.

Stinchcombe, A. (1965) "Social structures and organizations." In *Handbook of Organizations*, ed. J. G. March, pp. 142–93. Rand McNally: Chicago.

Sutton, R. (1996) "Generalization in reinforcement learning: successful examples using sparse coarse coding." *Advances Neural Inference Process Systems*, 8: 1030–44.

Sutton, R. and A. Barto (1998) *Reinforcement Learning: An Introduction*. MIT Press: Cambridge, MA.

Szulanski, G. (1996) "Exploring internal stickiness: impediments to the transfer of best-practices within the firm." *Strategic Management Journal*, 17: 27–43.

Teece, D. (1986) "Profiting from technological innovation: implications for integration, collaboration, licensing, and public policy." *Research Policy*, 15: 285–306.

Teece, D. (2007) "Explicating dynamic capabilities: the nature and microfoundations of (sustainable) enterprise performance." *Strategic Management Journal*, 28: 1319–50.

Teece, D., G. Pisano, and A. Shuen (1997) "Dynamic capabilities and strategic management." *Strategic Management Journal*, 18(7): 509–33.

Teece, D. J., R. Rumelt, G. Dosi, and S. G. Winter (1994) "Understanding corporate coherence: theory and evidence." *Journal of Economic Behavior and Organization*, 23: 1–30.

Tesuaro, G. and T. Sejnowski (1989) "A parallel network that learns to play Backgammon." *Artificial Intelligence*, 39: 357–90.

Thorndike, E. (1899) "The associate process in animals." Biological Lectures from the Marine Biological Laboratory Woods Hole Atheneum.

Trigeorgis, L. and J. Reuer (2017) "Strategic management and real options." *Strategic Management Journal*, 38: 42–63.

Tushman, M. L. and E. Romanelli (1985) "Organizational evolution: a metamorphosis model of convergence and reorientation." In *Research in Organizational*

Behavior, ed. L. L. Cummings and B. M. Staw, pp. 171–222. JAI Press: Greenwich, CT.

Tushman, M. L. and P. Anderson (1986) "Technological discontinuities and organizational environments." *Administrative Science Quarterly,* 31(3): 439–65.

Twain, M. (1897) *Following the Equator.* Sun-Times Publishing: Chicago.

Van Maanen, J. (1973) "Observations on the making of policemen," *Human Organization,* 32: 407–18.

Vanneste, B. (2017) "How much do industry, corporation, and business matter, really? A meta-analysis." *Strategy Science,* 2: 121–39.

Vaughan, D. (1996) *The Challenger Launch Decision.* The University of Chicago Press: Chicago.

Von Hippel, E. (1988) *The Sources of Innovation.* MIT Press: Cambridge, MA.

Weick, K. (1979) *The Social Psychology of Organizing,* 2nd ed. Addison-Wesley: Reading, MA.

Whittle, P. (1988) "Restless bandits: activity allocation in a changing world." *Journal of Applied Probability,* 25: 287–98.

Williamson, O. (1975) *Markets and Hierarchies, Analysis and Antitrust Implications: A Study in the Economics of Internal Organization.* Free Press: New York.

Williamson, O. E. (1985) *The Economic Institutions of Capitalism.* Free Press: New York.

Winter, S. G. (1964) "Economic 'natural selection' and the theory of the firm." *Yale Economic Essays,* 4(1): 225–72.

Winter, S. G. (1987) "Knowledge and competence as strategic assets." In *The Competitive Challenge: Strategies for Industrial Innovation and Renewal,* ed. D. Teece, pp. 159–83. Ballinger Press: Cambridge, MA.

Winter, S. G. and G. Szulanski (2001) "Replication as a strategy." *Organization Science,* 12: 730–43.

Winter, S. G., G. Szulanski, D. Ringov, and R. Jensen (2012) "Reproducing knowledge: inaccurate replication and failure in the franchise organization." *Organization Science,* 23: 672–85.

Wright, S. (1933) "Evolution in Mendelian genetics." *Genetics,* 16: 97–159.

Wry, T., M. Loundsbury, and M. Glynn (2011) "Legitimating nascent collective identities: coordinating cultural entrepreneurship." *Organization Science,* 22(2): 449–63.

Wu, B., Z. Wan, and D. Levinthal (2014) "Complementary assets as pipes and prisms: innovation incentives and trajectory choice." *Strategic Management Journal,* 36: 1257–78.

Index

For the benefit of digital users, indexed terms that span two pages (e.g., 52–53) may, on occasion, appear on only one of those pages.